BORN TO WALK

BORN TO WALK

MY JOURNEY
of TRIALS and RESILIENCE

Alpha Nkuranga

Edited by Jill Ainsley.
Copy edited by Candida Hadley.
Cover and page design by Julie Scriver.
Cover photograph of Alpha Nkuranga by One for the Wall Photography.
Maps by Marcel Morin, Lost Art Cartography.
Printed in Canada by Marquis.
10 9 8 7 6 5 4 3 2 1

Library and Archives Canada Cataloguing in Publication

Title: Born to walk : my journey of trials and resilience / Alpha Nkuranga.
Names: Nkuranga, Alpha, author.
Identifiers: Canadiana (print) 20240351088 | Canadiana (ebook) 20240351258 |
ISBN 9781773103341 (softcover) | ISBN 9781773103358 (EPUB)
Subjects: LCSH: Nkuranga, Alpha. | LCSH: Nkuranga, Alpha—Childhood and youth. |
LCSH: Rwanda—History—Civil War, 1994. | LCSH: Victims of family violence—
Rwanda—Biography. | LCSH: Rwanda—Social conditions—20th century. |
LCSH: Immigrants—Canada—Biography. | LCSH: Resilience (Personality trait) |
CSH: Rwandan Canadians—Biography. | LCGFT: Autobiographies.
Classification: LCC DT450.437.N58 A3 2024 | DDC 967.57104/31092—dc23

Goose Lane Editions acknowledges the generous support of the Government of Canada,
the Canada Council for the Arts, and the Government of New Brunswick.

Goose Lane Editions is located on the unceded territory of the Wəlastəkwiyik
whose ancestors along with the Mi'kmaq and Peskotomuhkati Nations signed
Peace and Friendship Treaties with the British Crown in the 1700s.

Goose Lane Editions
500 Beaverbrook Court, Suite 330
Fredericton, New Brunswick
CANADA E3B 5X4
gooselane.com

FSC
www.fsc.org

MIX
Paper | Supporting
responsible forestry
FSC® C103567

For Mama and my children, Isaac, Jonathan, and Nathan.
And for Buseka.

We talk about love, but do we really show it?

Content Note:

This memoir contains true accounts of intimate-partner violence, violence toward children, war, and sexual harassment.

Contents

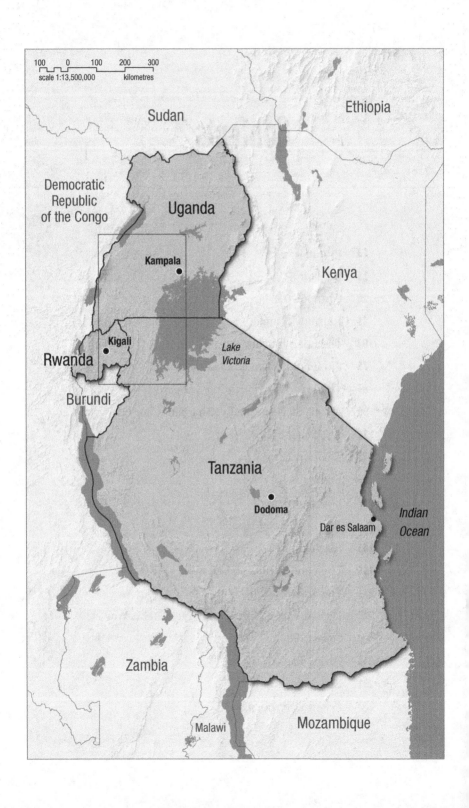

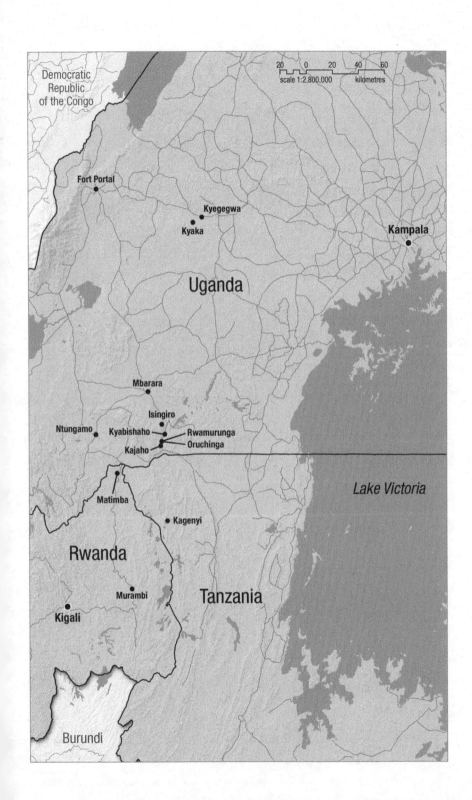

Prologue

They have a saying where I was born, "God sleeps in Rwanda." My grandparents used to tell me Rwanda is a country unlike any other, and I knew they spoke the truth. It is one of the few countries on the African continent where all citizens speak one language, Kinyarwanda. Blessed with majestic mountains and breathtaking valleys, it is a sacred and spiritual land, and Rwandans carry the belief that God loves Rwanda more than any country in the world. And yet Rwandan men drenched the land in blood in acts of hate so horrific that the stains of those three years will not fade in one hundred lifetimes.

My story is not an easy one to share. Although I come from a storytelling culture, I have long tried to heal myself through dissociation from the events of my past. From time to time, I've shared an experience or two with friends or my husband, my closest friend. But the past pierces my broken heart like a spear. It is easier not to share. And yet I am. Friends have encouraged me to tell my truth. I want to tell this story for the people who died and for their children, and especially for the women from back home. Because I survived, I can share what happened to us.

This is my story, told as I remember it, but it is not the whole story. Some parts are still too painful for me to share.

ONE

Imigani

I don't know the date or year of my birth; it was never recorded. My mother gave birth to me at home. I was her third child, and it was only when someone told her that she looked pregnant that she knew she was expecting me. A few months later, she unexpectedly went into labour. She had given birth to my older brother and sister at her parents' house because my grandmother was renowned for her midwifery skills, and Mama intended to travel to my grandparents' place for her third baby, but I was born early. Because my mother didn't know how to read or write, she had no way of documenting the dates of our births. The only sense I have of my birthday is from her saying, "I remember when you were born. It was morning, and it was raining." While I cannot know for certain, I believe that when the Rwandan Civil War happened in 1994, I was eight years old.

In my culture, fathers named their children. My father chose Irafasha for me, but in our community, people called you what they liked based on your behaviour and appearance. For example, if you were short, someone might call you Ball, and if you had a loud voice, another person might call you Thunder. Some called me Short because I was short. Others called me Miracle. There were many other names as well.

My mother called me Lucky because I never caused her any trouble during her pregnancy. She told me that I was very healthy for a week-old baby. I had a strong neck compared to other babies, and I developed so quickly that she intentionally hid me from the neighbours. Our culture is both superstitious and wary of anything that appears out of the ordinary. She wanted to prevent people from seeing me as abnormal.

At about a month old, I attempted to sit without support from anyone. To discourage me from sitting at an age thought to be too young, she kept me wrapped up and carried me on her back using a wrapper, made from one of Africa's traditional fabrics. One day, when I was around four months old, I was lying on the bed while my older brother, Bosco, was playing in the same room. He turned around and saw that I was sitting by myself. He rushed to call our mother. When she saw me, I was sitting up and giggling to myself. She immediately stopped me and ordered my brother not to tell anyone about it.

At five months, I was standing on my feet despite my mother's efforts to keep me sitting. She was shocked because most babies don't start walking until about ten months. At six months, I was running. My mother then had to stop me from going outdoors, fearful that people would think I was a cursed child. She cleaned the house, fetched water, cooked, and gardened with me on her back. She left me alone only during nap time and bedtime when everyone was asleep and she knew no one would see me walking.

My mother tried her best to hide it, but I had been kugenda munda, born walking. Every day, my feet were on the ground, ready to go somewhere. Because I started walking at such a young age, one of the names bestowed on me was Akaduri, which meant short walker. In time, this was shortened to Kadur, and it was the name I was most commonly called.

As a child, I walked so much that my feet sometimes cracked and bled. Eventually the soles became hard as stone. Perhaps even then God was preparing me for what lay ahead.

My mother is a brown-skinned woman, darker than me, with short hair and a birthmark next to her right eye. She has always been quiet and loving with a humble, contemplative disposition. When she stands, she stands with her back straight. Recently I asked her how she met my father, and she told me that one day, when she was a teenager, she was out walking when my father and his friends took her away and he raped her. Later, he took her a second time, and this time she became pregnant. She married my father. She had no other choice. She risked being killed for shaming her family if she refused. The word *guterura* means to lift or carry something, but to young women in our culture, it has a more sinister meaning. If a man becomes interested in a girl and her parents refuse his request to marry her, the man might recruit someone to stalk her day and night, waiting for a moment when she's alone. At an opportune moment, they strike, gagging her with a cloth and taking her by force far from her family. The next morning, she wakes up married to a stranger, nursing wounds suffered during the abduction and rape. Guterura, the practice of forcible marriage, would touch my life more than once.

When my mother was pregnant with her firstborn, my brother Bosco, she was sickly and weak. All she could eat was clay. In my culture, when a woman gives birth, her parents will take care of her for the first two months after childbirth. Someone else takes charge of caring for the newborn so the mother has ample time to heal and recuperate. Once the baby is born, many of the father's relatives will come to see if the baby resembles its father. If the baby does not, those mothers will have to stay forever in their parents' house, as their husbands will never come for them. It's not a good way to verify paternity since newborns sometimes don't resemble either parent. Luckily for my mother, she had very few in-laws interested in checking up on her newborn son.

Babies remain nameless for several days until the father shows up with an official name. Naming ceremonies are a big deal. Friends and members of the extended family gather to celebrate, bringing money and other gifts for the mother and her baby. For the new mothers, the ceremonies celebrate their survival from the ordeal of childbirth. Despite the skills of midwives like my grandmother, many childbirths result in the death of the mother or the baby, and sometimes both. If a baby dies during labour, the mother is blamed for failing to push it out. Labouring women are sometimes flogged to get them to push.

My father is a tank in physical form — and in disposition. Rwandan men are supposed to be tough. There is a saying in Kinyarwanda, "Amarira yu'mugabo atemba Agana Munda" — "Tears of men flow inside." I can't remember ever seeing a man in Africa cry. My father has always carried himself as someone capable of causing harm. His face is the face of someone hostile to the world. When he was young, the villagers nicknamed him Ingwe Muntu, the Human Leopard. Our village was in northern Rwanda, near the forest, and houses in this area were prone to attacks from wild animals. One morning, my father and his brother were out walking. Near a tall ant hill, they found a leopard that had been caught in a trap. Even though it was injured and trapped, the leopard was still able to jump on my father. It dug its claws into his skull. He threw it against the ant hill, but the leopard attacked again. My father fought it while his brother ran for help. Some police with guns were nearby and came to assist, but they couldn't shoot for fear of hitting my father. By that time, so much blood covered him that no one could have recognized him.

Some say the two continued to fight for an hour; others say it was two hours. Finally, one of the men was able to shoot the leopard. My father spent a long time in Kiziguro Hospital, recovering from several surgeries. People said he was the first man ever to win a battle with a leopard. He won the title of the village's strongest man, and people feared him so much that no one would even touch his arm. To this day, my father wears this battle on his body. He has a large indentation in his skull, so large that it is clear to me that he suffered some sort of brain damage, and several long scars across the top of his head. He has gone through life bullying and forcing his will on other people, particularly my mother, who has never been able to escape him or his anger. All my life, he's been prone to rages that cause my family to flee the house. At one point, he kept three long machetes under his bed. People are generally allowed to keep machetes because they use them for bushwhacking and other practical purposes, but my father threatened to kill my mother with them. The police confiscated the machetes, and I asked a village elder to try to reason with my father, to get him to change his violent ways, but to no avail. Whenever my mother leaves him, she always returns, and I remain fearful for her safety.

My mother had ten children all together: six before the war and another four after. I am the third child. I have one older brother and five younger, and three sisters, one older and two younger. Bosco, the first child, was around eight or nine years older than me and was nicknamed Brown because of his smooth brown skin. My older sister, Uwimpuhwe, is two years my senior. She is thin and tall with light skin. My sister Godance was born three years after me. She looks a lot like my mother. She was always my good friend when we were growing up. My other siblings are my brother Elijah, my sister Sharitina, and my youngest brothers, Nani, Joseph, and Friday.

My parents were living in Murambi, a small city in southern Rwanda, when Bosco was born. When he was young, they moved north to the village of Rugarama, a relatively new rural settlement near the forest and not far from the Tanzanian border, to have more space to raise their family. The trading centre for this tiny village was in Matimba. Rugarama was composed of small pockets of acreages among rolling green hills and winding dirt roads. Most houses were rectangular or square and made of mud with grass roofs. People who had more money roofed their homes with iron sheets. Most houses had doors made of wood with barrel bolts to lock them shut. The houses were spaced far apart, and it would often take ten or fifteen minutes to walk from one house to another.

On our acreage we had chickens and goats close by, while our cows grazed farther away in the fields. Christianity was a big part of my life. Our church was built with mud and had an iron roof. Inside were rows of traditional Rwandan church chairs made of mud and backless wood benches.

When I was young, my father deserted us for other women because after giving birth to my brother Bosco, my mother's next three children were girls. When my sisters and I married, he would exchange us for cows or other valuable products, but a one-time dowry was nothing compared to sons who would inherit his land and other properties. He took a second wife, Dorosera, and began having children with her, but he also returned to my mother whenever he wanted. She gave birth to my younger brother, Elijah, when I was around four, and my father continued to come and go as he pleased. My father's long absences made it difficult for my mother to care for all of her children, and from time to time she would send Elijah and me to live with our paternal aunt and grandparents in Murambi, a trip of about an hour and half by taxi.

Although I am Rwandan by birth, I grew up more fluent in Runyankore, the language of the Ankole people from Western Uganda, because when I was very young, my mother sent me to Uganda to live with my father's sister Karuhanga. I didn't return to Rwanda to see my parents and maternal grandparents until I was around six years old, and in the years before the Rwandan Civil War, I often returned to Uganda for extended periods. Crossing the border was easy then.

I grew up surrounded by beautiful and imaginative storytellers who passed down to us all of our history. I was taught to listen carefully and remember the words. One voice in particular still rings in my ears, that of my aunt Karuhanga. In my culture, paternal aunts play an enormous role in raising children and in teaching girls the way of women. They are the caretakers of girls' morality. But Aunt Karuhanga was much more than a storyteller, guardian, and instructor in how to survive in a world created for men. She opened my mind and empowered me to think about and reflect on what is true for me. Her patient face, calm, searching eyes, heavy eyelids, prominent cheekbones, and healthy inner power embodied wisdom drawn from an inexplicable source.

When memory glides me down the rivers of my past, I see myself, a young girl, joyfully sitting on her lap with her arms wrapped around my waist. When she visits my dreams, I am relieved to hold her until I wake up. No matter the distance between us or how long we are apart in this life, she has a permanent place in my heart. She receives my love with every beat and will do so until the end of my time. I admire her loving spirit. I have trained myself to speak and to walk like her.

Before the Rwandan Civil War, my ethnically mixed family, like many others, met and told stories by the fire, a practice called imigani. The fireplaces of my youth were rock circles laid on the ground outside our homes, which allowed every family member to sit around the fire, connected to each other. At the fireplace my family found communion. The questions of the children prompted the elders to teach generational lessons through parables and proverbs, and we paid careful attention, knowing they would ask us to recall these stories later. Many of the stories privileged and protected the patriarchal culture in which we lived. Goat meat was considered delicious, and men sought to retain it for themselves, so young girls were taught that eating goat meat would give them beards and make them undesirable. My aunt inculcated this patriarchy in my mind and in the minds of my sisters and girl cousins. We were taught the proverb, "Ukandagira agahungu ntahonyora" — "Don't step on a boy or treat him badly," because he will remember and may use it against you when he grows up. Educated people never surrounded me, but I was raised by intelligent women with significant life experience.

When we gathered at the fire for imigani, the boys sat on traditional chairs. Boys, after all, were future men. The women and girls sat on mats on the ground. I would sit beside Aunt Karuhanga on a mat we had made together from cattail grass we picked ourselves in nearby swamps. We would strike the long grass with rocks until they softened and then dry them for two days in the sun. When they were drained of colour and moisture, we wove them across string to make mats and baskets. It was special to us that during our family time around the fireplace, we enjoyed imigani on mats that we made with our hands from grass we pulled from our land.

Our fireside storytelling was always outside. During the day, my siblings and I collected the wood and sometimes dried cow dung, which we burned to keep the mosquitoes away. During the rainy season, when fires outside were not possible, we would host story time in the heartbeat of our home, our kitchen. For those occasions, I would cover my tiny body with my aunt's kitenge, a traditional and well-respected cloth typical in Congo, Nigeria, and Ghana but rarely worn in Ankole culture. Ankole women are known for their traditional dress called ekyitambi, a dress composed of a halter top and a wraparound skirt that slides on a flat braided rope worn around the waist. A large train of fabric is wrapped across the shoulders and bosom.

We always anticipated the beginning of stories and sometimes knew which ones could be told in a single sitting. Most of the time, we would listen to stories that were parts of a longer story. The storyteller would speak about a specific topic to teach a particular lesson or would choose what to say based on what was appropriate for the audience at hand. Knowing that we were only hearing piecemeal parts of a longer story created immense suspense. Those were stories my aunt would tell in parts, in different gatherings. I wish I could meet her again to learn how some of those stories ended!

Our story time usually started with a prayer, and midway into the tale, my aunt would call our names to see if we were engaged. She was illiterate, but she was the smartest teacher I have ever met. She taught me the importance of paying attention to what was said so I would become a critical observer of my world. While other kids were beaten if they did not pay attention, my aunt had more cunning and motivating methods. She would tell me to pay attention because if she later asked me what was taught and I didn't remember, I would be forbidden from hearing stories for two to three days, something I desperately wanted to avoid. I never wanted to miss out on the special things. I always listened with rapt attention, legs crossed as was the custom for girls. The questions that I as a young girl asked by the fire were about the origins of the stars and the moon. I thought that maybe one day I would study math or accounting so that I could count all the stars in the sky.

Surrounded by friends and family members, we would eagerly wait for my maternal grandmother and grandfather to recount our beautiful shared history and for my paternal aunt to tell us about her mother, Nyirabapira Veronic, my paternal grandmother. Her life profoundly shaped my views on belonging, survival, and motherhood, and affected how I now mother.

"It's very hard to give you a clear picture of your paternal grandmother," my aunt said when she recounted her mother's history. "But she left a legacy in Remera." Remera is now a suburb of Kigali, Rwanda's capital city, but during colonialism, when Rwanda was under Belgian rule, Remera was a mining town for cassiterite, the primary ore used to make tin. Any place associated with white people meant jobs and opportunity.

My grandmother Veronic had golden-brown skin and was tall and fat; in my tribe, everyone cherished chubby women and viewed slim women as ugly. Women are supposed to be the pillows for men to lie on. If a man rests his head on a thin woman's shoulder, he will be uncomfortable. A fat woman with big arms and legs is comfortable and sexy. Women in Rwanda and Uganda like to wear dresses that show the thickness of their arms, and they try many different ways to get fat, such as gorging on cow's milk.

Gramma Veronic challenged traditions. She wore a bra and spoke French at a time when speaking the white man's language was uncommon. Her ability to converse in an official language of the colonists elevated her position in the village, and she fell in love with a Belgian who had settled in Remera and became a prominent figure. When Veronic and the Belgian suitor broke the news of their courtship to her parents, they welcomed it as good news. They told the man to return in a few days, after the family had time to discuss the dowry and make the wedding arrangements. He planned to return to Belgium soon and was eager to hasten the process. He declined traditional marriage arrangements, urging Veronic's parents to tell him how many cows they wanted in exchange for their daughter so they could be married right away. The marriage took place within a few days, and he left for Belgium. His new wife soon followed him.

Veronic left everything and everyone she knew to become one of the first Rwandan women to live in Belgium, despite her low background. Soon after she reached Belgium, she gave birth to a handsome boy (I do not know his name). When her baby turned two, she became pregnant with a second boy, whom they named Dorom. But as days passed into weeks, it became increasingly clear that Veronic's husband had no paternal interest in his second son. Finally, Veronic asked him why he seemed so detached from his baby. He told her that he believed Dorom couldn't be his son because Dorom's skin was so dark. Veronic insisted that she had never been with any other man, but her husband didn't believe her.

Skin colour was, and perhaps still is, one of many status markers in my culture. The lighter the skin, the greater the status. One of the implications of colonization was the widespread perception that lighter skin denotes power: it was light-skinned colonizers who hammered the

African people into submission. Veronic was lighter than most of her family members. I can only guess that her firstborn son also had very light skin, and her husband assumed that all of his children would have that colouring. (In my own family, my siblings and I have different skin tones. People used to doubt that my brother Bosco and I came from the same parents because his skin is so much lighter than mine.) The Belgian refused to raise this child and present him to people as his own, and with that Veronic's dreams of happiness were whisked away like clouds in a fast-moving wind. Her in-laws made it clear that they would not help her, and she was thousands of miles from home. She had no one who could appeal to her husband on her behalf.

Her husband gave her a choice that never ceases to appall and bewilder me: kill Dorom and stay in Belgium or leave her firstborn in Belgium and take Dorom back to Rwanda. I think the Belgian assumed that she would choose him and life in Belgium over the burdensome child with browner skin. But Veronic's instinct to protect her baby prevailed, and without a second thought, she chose the latter option.

A few weeks later, her husband ordered her to pack what she wanted to take with her. She packed everything she could fit, including her kitchen utensils, bedsheets, and her clothes. He drove her to the airport, where she bade a tear-filled goodbye to her firstborn son, who was likely three years old at the time. It was a goodbye that would trouble her for the rest of her life. She never saw her boy again. When my aunt told the story, she said that for Veronic, leaving her firstborn felt like throwing herself into a grave while she was still breathing. For the rest of her life, she wondered about the fate of the child she left in Belgium.

Veronic spent the next two days on planes, wondering what everyone would think of her, scared to tell them that she gave up her firstborn. But when she reached Remera, she discovered that her parents had passed away and there was no one to comfort her.

Before she had married the Belgian, many villagers both envied Veronic because she had the privilege of choosing the man she wanted, something that was very unusual at that time, and despised her because her relationship with a colonialist gave her access to privileges denied to them. Before she left for Belgium, people joked about naming the town after her; when she returned without her husband, they ostracized her. The people of Remera did not see her as one of their own nor did they see a woman in pain. They only saw a modernized woman, the wife of the white man. She wore pants, forbidden in that society, and so they labelled her a prostitute. She also wore short dresses and skirts, and so they no longer called her a mother. Elders in the community condemned her style of dress and demanded that she change.

Dorom had chocolate skin and very soft, curly hair. Like Veronic, he faced discrimination. Because he was not born in Rwanda, he was not supposed to speak Kinyarwanda. A few days after Dorom turned eight years old, he suddenly became sick and died. Veronic believed someone in the village had poisoned him. Veronic had left her first son and her marriage to save Dorom's life, and now her village had killed him. She was hollow and devastated. When she met a man who promised to love her unconditionally, she married him. He already had a wife, but polygamy is accepted in our culture. Soon she gave birth to my dad, Nkuranga, and then to my aunts Karuhanga and Kamonyo.

Veronic always stood out. She was the first in the village to use cooking pots instead of handmade pots, called inkono. Poverty makes people very jealous. Where I come from, people don't want to see others succeed. The more materially successful you are, the more your life is at risk, and many people who know they are envied sleep with one eye open. When my aunt Kamonyo was about eight years old, Gramma Veronic, like her son Dorom, died of a sudden illness that suggested poison. (Years later, when my infant son became ill during a trip to Uganda, the fear that he'd been poisoned would cross my mind.)

Veronic's story stood out to me when I was a child because her struggles were unlike any I had ever known, and yet I could understand the choices she made. I knew even then that I wanted the threads of her experiences to be part of the tapestry of my own experience. Through her sad story I learned a series of life lessons. My grandmother's decision to take her baby and leave one behind has taught me to value my children and stay resilient through difficult times. Every time I experience challenges in my relationship, I remember her bravery and determine to work harder to overcome the odds for my children, but I also know that I can survive if I ever need to leave my partner.

None of those who killed my grandmother are still alive. I don't have an answer as to why people choose to hate instead of loving each other when our time here is so short. This world is not our home.

TWO

Girlhood

I learned what it meant to be a girl in a patriarchal culture at a very young age. Evidence that boys were more valuable than girls surrounded me. I was not permitted to be myself, to learn through growing. Instead, my whole life was filled with one prohibition after another. Boys sat on chairs; girls sat on traditional mats. Boys learned how to build houses and tend to the garden and livestock; girls learned to sweep and cook. While girls were expected to learn only how to read and write, boys were encouraged to go as far as they could in school. Girls were married off in their early teens, but boys married in their late teens and twenties. A girl's family usually chose her husband while boys had more freedom to choose their wives. In Ankole culture, women get down on their knees to greet a man or serve him food, and when they serve him food, they bring him a basin so he can wash his hands first. This is how they show him respect, and if they refuse, they are labelled bad women with poor manners. It doesn't take long for boys to learn their inherent superiority to girls and women.

It wasn't just that we weren't allowed to eat goat meat. Parts of the chicken were also off limits. They belonged to the man, the king of the house. Once I was at Karuhanga's house and she cooked tilapia. I loved fish. All day I watched the red soup boiling in the pot and my stomach rumbled in anticipation. I thought about dipping mashed matooke in the soup to scoop up a piece of fish. I couldn't wait until it was time to eat.

When the food was ready, we all sat in a circle. We sat on the ground. In our culture, men do not eat with the rest of the family, so my uncle sat at his table, alone. My aunt served the food. She put three pieces of tilapia on his plate but served everyone else only soup. The other children ate their soup and went to wash their hands. I stayed in my place, waiting for fish.

"Go and wash your hands," my aunt said.

"I'm waiting for fish."

"Sorry, darling," she said. "Only the man eats fish. The rest of the family just gets soup."

I burst into tears. My aunt held me tightly to her chest. She wasn't upset that I couldn't eat the fish. She was upset that she couldn't explain to me *why* I couldn't eat the fish.

I loved eating pawpaw, avocado, and mangoes. I was also skilled at climbing trees. Climbing was only for boys, but no one could explain to me why an adventurous girl should not climb, and even though my paternal aunt, who was responsible for training me, had warned me not to climb trees, I did not listen. One day my cousin and I went to a plantation to pick fruit. I told him to have a seat and I would throw some mangoes down to him. But, remembering a previous trip when my cousin had climbed a banana tree but did not share the fruit he picked with me, I decided that I would not share with him.

I climbed up high, plucked a ripe mango, and gave it a big, juicy bite. Far below my cousin sat staring at me, expecting that I would throw a mango to him, but instead I picked a second and started eating. He opened his palm and begged, saliva drooling from his mouth. "Throw one to me!" he said. After a few more bites, I told him I would not share, reminding him about the bananas. In my mind, I was doing him a favour. Depriving him of mangoes would teach him how I felt when he wouldn't share with me. Maybe he would change his ways. After filling my belly, I heard Aunt Karuhanga's thundering voice.

"Come down!" she shouted. "Come down, right now!"

My heart started racing. She carried a big stick, and that meant I was in trouble. I started crying and promised I would never climb trees again.

"Come down," she said again.

As I made my way through the branches, I hoped she would not beat me and vowed that I would never again make the mistake of climbing a tree to get mangoes, no matter how much I loved them.

"Today is going to be a day you will never forget," my aunt said when I reached the ground. "I am very sure that you will never climb trees again! Lie down."

My cousin was giggling in the background. I lay clutching handfuls of dirt and steadying myself for the beating, praying that she would give me one last chance. My aunt always gave us three warnings before she punished us, but she'd already given me three warnings, and I was sure I could not escape a thrashing. But then a reprieve! "Let us call it a lucky day for you," she said. I let out a deep sigh of relief, thanking God for saving me. Her threats were enough. That was the last day I ever climbed a tree for fun. Looking back, I don't think my aunt really believed that climbing trees was wrong, but she knew that if she didn't try to break me of the habit, people would accuse her of not raising me properly.

Our paternal aunts made sure girls knew to keep their virginity until marriage and, once married, to never reject their husband's demands for sex. They also taught every girl that she should never raise her voice to her husband and should always support and care for him. The community revered female virginity as a woman's sacred gift to her husband, and if a young woman remained a virgin until marriage, her aunt would receive gifts, such as beautiful cloth, in appreciation. But if a new husband discovered that his bride was not a virgin, he would rip a hole in the bedsheet and send it to her aunt, implying that the girl received improper training. Boys, of course, were not held to this standard.

Although female genital mutilation is not practised in Rwanda, the culture does not permit girls to enjoy their bodies. Ankole culture and Rwandans pull the labia minora to make them as long as possible. "Pulled" girls are considered more marriageable, and approximately 98 per cent of girls experience this practice. A group of teenage girls will heat up an intobo fruit and then apply the juice to the labia. The juice is very itchy and causes the genitals to swell and the skin to loosen. Then the girls pull the skin like they are milking cows. This is repeated until the labia is the length of a grown woman's middle finger. It's an excruciatingly painful procedure and makes walking difficult, especially when pants and other garments rub against the stretched labia, causing chafing and irritation. Pulling not only permanently transforms the genitalia but reduces sensation during intercourse.

I saw women beaten by their husbands — including my quiet and loving mother — and yet nobody talked about it. I didn't know anyone empowered or brave enough to change the ways women were treated in our society, but I often wondered about the value of womanhood. If God knew that women would be considered inferior and treated like slaves, why did He create them?

My mother had a younger sister, Janet. She was my aunt, but because she was only a few years older than me, we grew up together. One evening after a dry and humid day, we went to fetch water from the well near the swamp. The best times to get water or collect firewood were either early in the morning or just after sunset, when it was sunny but not scorching and fewer people were in the swamp, which meant the water wouldn't be too churned up. I was about seven years old and Janet would have been around eleven. I carried a half-sized jerrycan. On this evening, I was in a hurry because I wanted to play with my friends.

My favourite game was one that I thought Rwandans had created; it was only much later that I learned that it's called hide and seek and is played by children all over the world. We had so much fun hiding in the tall grass and exploring nooks and crannies in the land. I especially loved playing this game after the bean harvest in May, when I would bury myself completely inside the dried beans so nobody could see me, even when the seekers were standing so close I could reach out and touch them. After ten minutes of searching, the seekers would shout "Tanga agatego!" to let me know they gave up and I could announce myself as the winner. My reward was that someone else would do my chores, like fetching water.

The well was about a half hour's walk from the houses. Janet and I were midway to the well when we noticed two men who looked to be in their early twenties behind us. We ignored them.

Shortly after we started filling our jerrycans, the men approached us. They threatened to throw Janet into the swamp if she disobeyed their orders. I was terrified and confused, and Janet started to cry. They dragged Janet to a nearby tree, one pulling while the other pushed. She struggled to get free, but they overpowered her.

I dropped my jerrycan and ran faster than the wind. My heart hammered in my chest and sweat ran down my back as I pushed myself to keep running, harder and harder, to get home. I kept looking back to see if someone was after me. I stumbled and fell more than once, but each time, I jumped up and ran even faster. When I reached home, my maternal grandfather was sitting on one of the traditional chairs, making a beehive.

"Janet, Janet, Janet!" I screamed.

"Where is she?" my grandfather asked. "Where is she?" He must have thought she had fallen in the well and drowned. The only thing I could say was her name, over and over again. I could not have explained because I didn't understand what was happening. I just knew it was very bad.

We ran together, and when we reached the well, my grandfather went to see if Janet had drowned, but I kept pointing at the tree. I couldn't see the men; they must have heard us coming and run away. Janet was dishevelled and covered with grass, but she was alive. She had tears in her eyes, but she only started crying when we reached home.

My grandparents blamed Janet for what had happened to her. They warned her to shut her mouth or forget about marriage, since no one would marry a woman who had lost her virginity. They scolded her for wearing inappropriate clothes, saying she had attracted the rapists. No one stood up for Janet. Everyone just blamed her for failing to cover her legs.

Janet was her family's last born, and they had treated her like a queen. She could misbehave and nobody would punish her. My grandfather had a dedicated chair and place where he would sit and eat from plates that no one else could use. It was a special moment if he called you over to eat with him. He gave that privilege almost exclusively to Janet. She was the only one he allowed to eat the leftovers off his plate.

Things changed after the rape. Janet didn't share her feelings with me, but I could see the change in her and in her relationship with my grandparents. The extra love and care that Janet had enjoyed as a favoured child disappeared, and they began to treat her like they did everyone else. The attack scarred her deeply. She felt that no one liked her and no one outside the family would want her. Some years later, when she was around sixteen, she became pregnant. She had three more children, but she never formed a stable relationship. Janet became an alcoholic and a single mother, and two of her children eventually died. Many years later I saw her during a visit to Uganda, and she was yamfuye a hagaze, the walking dead. She lived in a haze and everyone, including her children, condemned her. One act of sexual violence turned her into a pariah.

Sexual violence was common in Uganda, too. I remember a day when I was playing outside with some other kids and it started to rain. I had laundry hanging up to dry, and I ran to get it inside. A little four-year-old girl I was playing with sought shelter in a neighbour's house. After I'd finished with my laundry, I went to the neighbour's house to look for her. The neighbour's son, a seventeen-year-old named Festo, said she wasn't there, but when I called her name, she answered. When I heard her voice, I knew something was wrong. My face flushed, and my heart began to pound. I pushed my way inside the house and found her, naked and bleeding. If I'd had a gun at that moment, I would have killed Festo.

I rushed the girl to the nurse, who confirmed that she had been sexually assaulted. The nurse could do nothing to fix what Festo had done to her but gave me some cream to help soothe her wounds. I told the neighbour what Festo had done, and Festo confessed to the rape. I threatened to tell the police. "What is the point of reporting this to the police?" my neighbour asked. "The police can't give her back what she lost, so just move on." Festo's father was rich, and even if I went to the police, I was told, Festo wouldn't spend a single night in prison.

I knew they were right. In Uganda, money talks. If you don't have money to bribe the police, there is no point in reporting a crime, and if you do report a crime and the perpetrator has more money than you to pay the police, you could be the one in trouble. I knew that I could not win this fight, and I decided that bringing attention to this little girl with no hope of change would result in a shame that would be worse for her than the assault itself.

These stories are not unique to Uganda, Rwanda, or Africa writ large. Globally, the subject of sexual and gender-based violence is not something our leaders want to discuss. We don't provide enough help for the victims whose lives are devastated, and too often, the perpetrators of such violence don't get the punishments they deserve. When you have clear evidence of a sexual assault and people excuse the perpetrator and blame the victim, the system is broken.

These experiences reinforced for me that women had no autonomy over their bodies. We couldn't even choose whom to marry. I remember well a conversation I had with my maternal grandmother, Kasine, about this.

I adored Kasine. She was uneducated, but she remains one of the smartest people I have ever met. She was famous in the village, well-respected and highly creative in making handicrafts. I spent countless hours learning from her because I wanted to be like her one day.

She was also a traditional midwife. People travelled from all corners of the country to be treated by her. Every morning, more than fifteen women assembled at her house for pregnancy checkups. She had a designated place that she used for delivering babies. She would wake up very early and search for traditional herbs for the pregnant women and sick people. Those on medication would stay at her house for days. People often gave her gifts of appreciation for her selfless services.

One day, a family came, carrying a pregnant woman in an ingobyi, a locally made rectangular-shaped carrier with handles on both sides. The family thought the woman was going to die and had carried her a great distance to see my grandmother. The baby's legs appeared before the head. I don't know how my grandmother changed the baby's position, but within a few minutes the crying family were drying their eyes and hugging one another with joy. An hour later, the baby was breathing perfectly. My grandmother had magic hands. When I asked her how she learned to do everything, she told me that her mother was a traditional midwife and passed on her knowledge. Her story inspired me, and I thought that one day I, too, would do something to change people's lives.

Kasine was tall and charming with long hair and flawless skin. But she had followed an old Rwandan beauty practice that required unmarried woman to sharpen their two front teeth and leave a small gap between them. One day, while we sat weaving traditional mats, I pointed to her teeth and teased, "Gram, I don't think you look so beautiful like that."

"People don't consider it beautiful these days," she replied. "But in my day, they did." I knew that when my grandmother was sixteen, she was married to a stranger chosen by her parents.

"I will never marry someone I don't know," I vowed.

"Those are the words for boys, my daughter," she replied. "Our society does not give you the right to choose a husband by yourself."

"I don't know about that," I said, "but I will fight for myself!" At that, my grandmother laughed so hard that tears flowed down her cheeks. I started laughing, too.

"Gramma, I am very serious," I continued. "I don't care what people will say about me, but I will marry the person I like."

Instead of trying to change my mind, she told me a story. "Do you see your uncle's wife?" she asked, referring to her daughter-in-law (in my language, we seek specificity; it is more clear to say "uncle's wife" than simply "aunt"). "Do you know how she got married?"

"No."

"I know many girls in this village who got married because men met them on the way going somewhere and took them just like that."

"Do you mean guterura?"

"Your parents might not force you to marry," my grandmother said, "but the boys may take you by force."

"Gramma, I don't care what people may say about me. I will never stand for a forced marriage. If they take me today or the next day, I will find ways to get out. I know the consequence: no one would ever marry me again."

My grandmother looked at me seriously. "My daughter," she said, "please make sure you don't disgrace us."

"It's my life!" I protested.

"You know marriage is essential in society," she said.

"I know, Gramma," I said. "But why does everything bad happen to girls and women and not men and boys? There is something wrong here, and people should solve it. Why can men marry the women they want, but women are not allowed to marry the men they want?"

"My daughter," she said, raising her voice. "These things have always been like this, even in my grandparents' time. Let me give you a piece of advice. One person cannot change the way society should run."

"That's why women should come together and fight the abuse against them!"

"Be careful," she said. "You will get into trouble. The family will kuguca you." *Kuguca* meant the family would disown me for misbehaving and nobody would be allowed to talk to me or give me anything. I would lose everything.

"I don't care," I said. "If I have to, I will go and live in another area." And I meant it from the bottom of my heart.

When I was very young, I thought that my grandmother loved my grandfather, but as time wore on, I observed that my grandmother lived in a separate part of the house. She did not cook for him, clean his clothes, or care for him when he was sick. I did not want to suffer the same fate. I wanted a relationship of mutual love and respect, where I cared for my husband and he cared for me. I knew that if my parents forced me to marry a stranger or a man I did not like, or if I married through guterura, *I* would become yamfuye a hagaze.

My Gramma Kasine was patient with me. She always listened carefully to my endless and often forthright questions. I knew others would not have been so tolerant. In my culture, speaking in public was prohibited for women. Everyone believed that outgoing women were likely to disrespect their husbands and discouraged women's self-expression. When a husband spoke to his wife, the wife was supposed to listen and then say, "Thank you, mutware (ruler)." I did not agree with this. I knew all the rules for girls and I resented them. I had a big dream: I wanted to go to school and study.

Girls weren't commonly encouraged to go to school. We were typically prepared for married life. Despite this, my mother decided it would be best for me to attend school in Uganda, where I could study in the language I was most comfortable with. And so, when I was eight, I prepared to say goodbye to my family in Rwanda. I could not have predicted the atrocities that lay ahead or how they would alter my entire life.

THREE

Kugenda Munda

April 1994. The sun was out, and it was a beautiful morning. In just a few weeks, I'd go to Uganda to start school, and my mother had sent me and my younger brother Elijah to stay with our maternal grandparents. Aunt Janet and I were playing behind the house. Gramma Kasine and Uncle Bugeni's wife were outside having their usual boring women's talk about why the girls in the family didn't listen and how they could better fulfill their caretaking roles. Our culture prohibited children from sitting with elders. If a visitor came to the house, the children had to go elsewhere. It was a way to prevent us from eavesdropping on adult conversations. But I could hear that Gramma was talking about a celebration she'd been invited to attend. Usually, Gramma would go alone and leave Janet and me at home to take care of the family. We knew that we would have to put everything back in the house and retire to bed after sunset.

While we were all outside, a neighbour came over and broke the news: rebels had caused a plane crash and the president of Rwanda had died. I did not care. I was raised to see life and death as part of a larger spiritual experience. In church, they told us that when a person dies, they immediately transition to living with God, and He will answer all the questions we always ask ourselves. I knew that when I died, I would miss my family, but being with Him would be the greatest experience. I had no way of knowing that the president's death would spark a series of events that would rain destruction upon our entire country.

Hutu extremists blamed Tutsi rebels for firing the missile that crashed the plane, killing President Juvénal Habyarimana and Cyprien Ntaryamira, the president of Burundi. They began killing the Tutsi people, and the Tutsi rebels started killing the Hutus in revenge (to this day, responsibility for the attack on these two presidents remains in dispute). My family was a mix of Hutu and Tutsi, and we never made distinctions along these lines. I knew my relatives as tall or short, with long noses or flat ones, dark skinned and others lighter skinned, and everyone spoke the same language. But one by one, family members began disappearing. In response to the Hutu killings of Tutsi, Tutsi rebels attacked and began killing everyone they encountered. My grandmother wanted to get me and Elijah back to our parents' house, but she soon learned this was impossible. Roadblocks were set up, and no one was allowed to travel. I was confused and scared, and none of the elders would tell me what was happening. Although I was not yet fluent in Kinyarwanda and did not understand everything people were saying, I picked up enough to know they were discussing the best place to take the children. Then the shouting turned to screams.

Desperate to get me and Elijah somewhere safe, my grandparents took us to my grandmother's relatives in Nyamatete, a village in eastern Rwanda. We stayed in Nyamatete for a few days before moving to another village and then another after that. Violence was everywhere. My grandparents decided to return to their village to see if it was safe.

We reached their home in the evening, near bedtime. Suddenly, we heard gunshots and the screams of people. Everyone scattered. I grabbed Elijah's hand, and we ran to the plantation. When we stopped running, I began to weep. I was confused and terrified. We were separated from the rest of the family. The steady rain just added to the chaos. And then, from somewhere, I heard a stranger's voice: "Keep quiet!"

Again I grabbed Elijah's hand, and we ran. The wet ground was slippery, and I fell repeatedly. Elijah started crying, and I closed his mouth with my hand. I was terrified of anyone hearing us. In the dark I had no idea where we were going. Finally, we found ourselves in the swamp. We waded into the water and stayed hidden all night. In the rainy season, the grasses are very long, and their density and height saved many people. I have often thought that many more would have perished if the fighting had broken out during the fall harvest.

I thought that when morning came, Elijah and I would find our family. But when the sun came up, I didn't hear people working or talking or any of the usual sounds of village life. The dissonance of the gunfire was our only company as bullets flew through the sky like birds. When we heard gunfire, we sank lower in the water. Smoke was everywhere, and I could hear large numbers of people being rounded up and forced into houses, and then I heard their screams when the rebels set fire to the houses. I had never experienced the death of a loved one. Death was hidden from children, but we were taught that when we died, we'd be reunited with our loved ones, so I did not associate death with pain. But the voices that rose with the smoke included at least ten people in my family. I also heard the voices of neighbours and playmates. This death I was hearing was far different from what I'd been taught. Hearing people I knew and loved scream for help as they died in one of the worst possible ways was completely outside my frame of understanding. This had never happened before in my culture; no story had prepared me for this moment.

Hearing visceral, howling death was one shock. The second shock was my own unfolding death. Lack of food left my body eating itself from the inside out. In the back of my mind I heard a loud, stern voice saying, "This is the end for you. You are nearing a death like you have never imagined."

Hidden in the swamp grasses, the steady hiss of insects in the quiet moments was deafening. The swamp smelled of decaying vegetation and rotten eggs. Snakes swam next to us but did us no harm. The true rebels lurked just outside, wielding machetes and guns. One night became three days. We had no food, and the only water we could drink was the rain we could catch in the palms of our hands and swamp water. After so long in the water, our skin turned white. We became bloated and itchy and began to cough. Fearful that the gunmen may hear us, I held my hand across my mouth to muffle my coughs. We used sign language to talk.

After the third day, Elijah lost the energy to cry. I could see that he was dying in my arms. In desperation, and determined to keep us alive if I could, I pulled up cattail stalks and fed him the roots. What instinct made me think to do that? I felt as if I were thirty years old.

For at least ten days, we ate cattail roots and drank water from our palms. We urinated and defecated in the swamp but drank from it, too. Many times, I thought about leaving the swamp, but Death was close to where we were hiding. Rising smoke blackened the sky above the village. I could hear screams and smell burning flesh. Much later, I learned that more than two hundred people, including some of my family, died in the fires of those early days. If God sleeps in Rwanda, where was He? Did He desert Rwanda for another country? These questions swam in my mind.

When I could no longer tolerate our agony, I came to the decision that we had to leave the swamp. Elijah was dying. My skin was diseased and itchy: pale white with scales like a fish. I vowed that the last thing I would do would be to eat matooke, an East African highland banana that I loved. And then, I heard some whispers close to us. I grabbed my brother's hand and moved slowly toward the voices. When they heard our footsteps, they froze with fear. I could tell that, like us, they had been hiding in the swamp for a long time.

"Do you have food?" I asked quietly.

"Who are you?"

"I am Kasine's granddaughter," I replied.

In a low voice, I told them about my family and how Elijah and I fled. We'd been hiding in the swamp for days, I said.

"We are sorry," one of them said. "We can't help you. We're heading to Tanzania, and it's a long journey. We're sorry that we can't take you with us."

They had uncooked cassava with them and gave one to my brother and me. At first, it seemed to be a tiny amount of food, but because we hadn't eaten in so long, after a few bites, I felt full, and my stomach ached. One of the men in the group agreed to help us get to Tanzania because he had recently lost his family. His told us his name was Buseka, and he volunteered to carry Elijah on his shoulders. I would have to walk.

We walked all night. It was dark and we could hardly see each other. I was terrified. I followed Buseka very closely because I was scared that I would lose my brother.

By morning, we were far from the terrors near the swamp, but I was exhausted. I could not feel any part of my body and didn't think I could make it. At noon, we stopped deep in the forest. We sat under the shade of the trees while some of the men hunted for food. We spent the rest of the day sleeping and recovering.

Soon, other groups joined us. Not everyone arrived unscathed. Some were bleeding, while others had lost body parts. I saw one woman with a piece of her neck almost falling off. She sobbed as she described how she lost her family — eight children beheaded in one day. She had pleaded with the murderers to kill her quickly, but they refused. Instead, they hacked a wound in her neck. They wanted her to bleed to death slowly. She told us that the killers were dressed in army uniforms and spoke a language different from Kinyarwanda. I had seen people cut the heads off cows, goats, and chickens, especially on Christmas Eve. It never entered my mind that people would behead other people.

The worst of the wounded people started dying. I had never seen someone take their last breath; I had never seen a dead person. I grabbed their hands and pleaded with them to wake up. Others told me to stop and leave the dead. We had to resume our journey.

My whole body burned with pain. I lost the nails on my swollen feet, and my toes bled. I crawled like a baby, and after a few hours, blood seeped from my palms. I prayed for death. I knew I was not going to reach Tanzania. Throughout the countryside, kids were dying like ants. I saw a mother lying on the ground, dead, while her baby still sucked at her breast. Nobody helped the baby. Parents deserted their children. I was a child. I could not save them, but I wept for them, and for myself and my brother, too. Everyone was trying to save their own lives. We were desperate.

I learned from the corpses I saw that when a person dies, their hair falls off after a few days. The smell of decomposing flesh made me vomit uncontrollably. I cursed the day God created human beings. Why did God let innocent people die, I wondered, especially pregnant women, infants and children, and older people? I kept pushing myself, but I felt like I was going nowhere. What would become of me?

In the evenings, we searched for wild fruits, tree roots, and pond water. We drank from the same sources that wild animals used, and it reeked of dung and tasted like urine. Every part of my body bled and throbbed with pain. Starvation left me thin and frail. When we stopped to rest, I sat on a big stone. I knew I could not continue. I could hear the roars of hungry lions around me, but I was ready for them to shred me to pieces. What was left to save? I thought of Aunt Karuhanga and Gramma Kasine. Who would pass on my story and the story of our family when I was gone? Elijah was too little.

A woman observed my exhaustion. "I don't think she can make it any farther," I heard her say. "We can leave her here. God knows that we tried our best."

"We are almost there," one of the men responded. "It's dangerous here. You can hear the lions. Let's encourage her for the last time. We can leave her in another place but not where hungry lions would eat her."

"Let's walk a little bit," the woman said to me encouragingly. "And when we reach a place without so many lions, we can take time to rest."

I had no strength to respond, but in my thoughts I blessed them, pushed myself up, and resumed walking.

We walked, and walked, and walked. We came to a mountain and began climbing. With each step, I hoped we would rest, but we never did. Tears flooded my cheeks, even though I knew that crying was not going to save me. That day, my tears did not stop. Finally, after hours of climbing, we reached the top of the mountain. It was very high, and the elders warned me not to look back.

"Look!" one of the men exclaimed. "We are close! Can you see that lake? We shall cross the lake and then reach Tanzania."

The night was fast approaching. Men, women, and children lay down under the trees and slept. I was always close to my brother. I didn't want anything to separate us in case I never saw him again. He was the only thing keeping me going. I tried to close my eyes, but the ground was hard and the pain was unbearable. Despite my exhaustion, some nights of that long journey I didn't close my eyes at all. I worried that someone would take Elijah away in the night.

The next morning, as usual, everyone searched for wild fruits for breakfast. After a few hours, we set off again, but this time, we could see where we were headed. By evening, we had reached the lake. We found many people waiting for boats to take them across the water. I had never seen a boat before. They were made from trees and could take four or five people at a time.

The boats belonged to sailors from Tanzania. We couldn't speak their language. As I sat on the shore, looking into the water, I saw three dead bodies floating close to the beach. They were tied together with a tree branch punched through their stomachs. I could tell by their pale and bloated skin that they had been in the water for many days. I didn't know if they were men or women; they had no hair on them, and it looked like they were going to burst. Once again, I struggled to understand how human beings could suffer to this extent.

A few minutes later, a boat returned, and the sailor asked which group was ready to go. To my shock, I learned that it was not a free ride. How did they expect us to pay? People pulled off their clothes — men offered their shirts and women their kitenge — in exchange for a trip across the lake. I had nothing but my dirty, blood-stained dress. I would be stranded on the shores of the lake.

As I listened to the sailors bargaining with the desperate passengers, I recognized a few words that sounded like Runyankore. Perhaps if I explained that Elijah and I were without parents and had nothing to bargain with, a sailor would take pity on us and let us travel for free. I watched as one boat after another filled with passengers. Finally the group we were travelling with was ready to board. Buseka, Elijah on his shoulders, beckoned me to follow him.

"Are they your kids?" the sailor asked him.

"Yes."

"Okay," the sailor said. "You can get in."

Relieved, I boarded the boat with Elijah.

It took us over an hour to reach our destination because the bodies floating in the water impeded the boats. The sailors had to hit some of them, breaking them into pieces so the boats could find a way through. It was nauseating. I swore to God that I, who loved meat and fish, would never again eat meat or fish.

Finally, we reached the opposite shore. We were safe in Tanzania! But our journey was not yet over. We had to travel to the Red Cross's reception station for refugees at the Kagenyi Camp. So we walked — one more time. We trudged for hours before we finally arrived at the camp. I couldn't believe my eyes. I thought almost no one had survived the massacres in Rwanda, but the camp was full of people. So many!

The Red Cross gave us porridge made from corn flour mixed with water and cooked until it bubbled and thickened. I was used to porridge made of millet and water. Corn-flour porridge, I quickly found, had almost no taste; it was like drinking warm water. The next day, Red Cross workers took us to an area of the camp where each family queued for registration.

Nobody had a complete family. Children had lost their parents; women had lost their husbands. Buseka suggested we register as a family with him. I was tempted, but my experiences had made me suspicious and fearful of men. If we registered as a family, we would be assigned to a single tent, and I could not help fearing that he would turn me into his wife. Buseka had done nothing to make me doubt him, but I had seen too much to trust him completely. When we reached the registration desk, I told them that Elijah and I were without a family.

I hoped this would mean that Elijah and I would be assigned to a tent together but near Buseka, but the Red Cross had designated a place for children without parents. I was reluctant to leave Buseka after everything he had done for us, but the registration official convinced me that I would see him again. "You will soon be back," the official said. "You are only going for your registration." So I grabbed my brother's hand and followed the volunteer. The official lied: we did not return, and I never saw Buseka again. I can never repay him for his help and kindness, but I know that he will be greatly rewarded, if not in this life, then the next. At a time when people committed unimaginable atrocities and thought only of saving themselves, Buseka, having lost his own family, looked at someone else's child and felt their pain. He was our Moses: Elijah would never have made it if Buseka had not carried him day after day, and he so often gave me words of encouragement when I needed them most. I hope that one day I find him again and tell him how grateful I am for what he did for us.

The camp was as crowded as an African market. It teemed with displaced men, women, and children. Many suffered with rotting gunshot wounds while others lay dying. A big tent housed a vast crowd of children without parents, and my brother and I joined the queue to register.

When it was our turn, the registration officer asked for my name.

I was confused, because I couldn't remember having an official name. I told the registration officer that my family would know me as Kadur. When he asked for my parents' names, I told him that I had been separated from my grandparents, not my parents.

"We need all the names of your family members," the registration officer said. "We will send your names to all camps in Africa and see if your parents are still alive."

This posed another problem for me. It was against our traditions for a child to call their parents by their proper names. I knew their names, but I constantly had to pretend that I didn't. I referred to the elders by their titles: Mama, Papa, Gramma, etc. Saying the names of our elders was so taboo that even at that moment I feared I'd get into trouble if I spoke them out loud. "I grew up not knowing the names of my parents," I lied.

"Well, there is no way we will find your parents without knowing their names," he said.

"I will tell you the names of my mama's parents," I said. "One is called Kaka, meaning grandma and another one is called Sogokuru, meaning grandfather."

Someone in the crowd shouted, "Girl, he is asking for their names!" Other voices yelled out, "Are you stupid?" I was causing a scene, and the Red Cross officials pulled me to the side. In the end, Elijah and I registered without providing the proper names of our parents.

Once we were registered, we were taken to a tent with other parentless children. The United Nations High Commissioner for Refugees (UNHCR) provided tents, blankets, clothing, and other household items. Boys and girls crowded together in one place. Diseases like dysentery, cholera, and kwashiorkor (caused by protein starvation) multiplied at an alarming rate. Children died in scores. I was covered in wounds and rashes, especially between my fingertips. Scabies and parasitic infections like jiggers made me so itchy that I thought it would drive me to madness. I scratched with sticks and rubbed my feet on the ground constantly to relieve the itch. Had I survived starvation and hungry lions only to die here? I wondered.

There is a saying in Kinyarwandan, "Aho gumfa uyumunsi nzamfe ejo" — "Instead of dying today, let me die tomorrow." We did what we could to stay alive for one more tomorrow. Unfortunately, the camps were not a safe place for girls. There were so many refugees and so few Red Cross workers in comparison. Girls were commonly raped, and men forced some girls into child marriages. The vulnerabilities that women and girls faced in such close quarters with thousands of desperate, idle men was almost unfathomable to me, and despite my young age I knew that I would be safer if people stopped seeing me as a girl. I had grown up knowing that boys got all the advantages and had sometimes wished that I had been born one. Adopting a boy's identity was my chance to enter a world that was otherwise denied to me. (It would never have crossed my mind that boys could be sexually assaulted, too.)

Boys and girls lined up separately to get clothes from UNHCR, and I simply joined the long line of boys. Elijah and I both received some pants and T-shirts, two or three items each. At first, the boys' clothes felt strange and uncomfortable to me, and I knew that pretending to be a boy would have been forbidden to me at home, but if it would keep me safe, I would be a boy. I wore boys' clothing all the time and played boys' games, too, especially football, and no one had any idea that I was a girl. When it was time to bathe with the other kids, I said that I had already had my bath. I skipped baths for weeks! Girls were vulnerable, but I felt safe because I was a boy. I was doing what I needed to see the next tomorrow.

I looked so much like a boy that when a traumatized and confused woman visited the camp, hoping to find her missing children, she mistook me for her son.

"Thank God!" she cried as she approached me. "I can see you again!"

"What?" I asked. "Who are you?"

"Baby, I am your mother!"

I was caught off guard. Uncertain how to respond to her, I simply fled. She chased me. I hid in a crowd of people. I was so small and skinny that she couldn't find me.

"I want my son!" she kept screaming. "I want my son!"

I could tell that she was disconnected from reality, so traumatized that she could no longer recognize the faces of her children. I imagined my mother going through the same trauma.

Life as a refugee meant living in queues. I lined up for everything. The children in the orphans' tent got food every day: porridge with oil in the morning, and lentils, corn, and beans for lunch and dinner. Sometimes UNHCR gave us expired beans, other times they handed out corn with mould in it. But we were lucky: families did not get food every day. Often they got only a couple of bags of lentils and dried corn twice a month. We also had to queue for clothing, wool blankets, jerrycans, medicine, and, if we were lucky, a weekly shower. Sometimes we would bathe in a nearby river. I, of course, couldn't bathe if people were around because I didn't want anyone to discover that I was a girl.

When we first arrived, Elijah and I slept on the ground in the open. Later, we shared a tent with other orphaned children. We slept on the dirt. Eventually we were given a blanket that we could cover ourselves with. Elijah was so young. I wondered if he understood anything that was happening to him. I always held his hand because I knew that if he ran away and I lost track of him, I would never find him again. The camp was a sea of people, and it was incredibly easy to get lost and never find your way back. I wondered if we would ever find our family. Death surrounded us. People we had grown accustomed to, our camp neighbours, died every day. I thought Elijah and I would be next. My only comfort was the knowledge that everyone around me was going through the same struggle for survival.

We were surrounded with children, and sometimes we would play and be joyful together, but most of the time we were just too sick. We would rest for long hours outside our tent while people passed us like we were in the middle of a market. In time, a rudimentary school was started under a tree, and this would busy us for a couple of hours a day.

Firewood was critical for survival, but getting it was difficult. People would collect firewood from the closest swamp, about ten minutes' walk from the camp, and also harvest cattail roots for cooking. Many drowned in the waters of the swamp.

I was sure that if the uncooked food did not kill me, I would die of viruses from drinking water contaminated with excrement. Anyone who needed to use the toilet would walk only a few metres behind the tent. When it rained, the excrement would run into the swamp where we collected our drinking and cooking water. The camp became survival of the fittest. I tried my best to stay healthy. I used herbs for the rashes on my body, but nothing worked. If my grandmother Kasine were with me, she would have done something to make my skin glow.

When I looked around, there were many things I didn't understand. Before the war, I ate fresh corn. I never learned to cook dried corn or cornmeal flour. Now dried corn was either prepared for us or I made it, something I learned by watching my neighbours. The Red Cross logo was scary to me. To me, red meant blood, and at first I wondered if the red cross meant they killed people. Of course I learned that the Red Cross offered help and support, and it was clear that they were kind-hearted people, but life in the refugee camp was miserable. More than once I suffered from dysentery. Scabies made my skin itch terribly, and kwashiorkor bloated my belly. I could hardly sleep at night, and I lay awake, always worried someone would kidnap Elijah. Traditionally, older kids are responsible for their younger siblings. Because my family trained me properly, it was ingrained in me to protect Elijah. I vowed I would, even if it meant I died trying. Sometimes I hoped we would find a family that would accept us and let us live with them. More than once I wished I could see Buseka again. I promised myself that if I found him, I wouldn't leave his side for even a second.

I don't believe you can live with death for so long and not think about the afterlife. When I was very young, I thought the dead left their graves at night and flew to the heavens to meet God. I remember the fear in my heart that a recently buried neighbour would come for me at night when I went to use the outside toilet. Burial, I believed, was the only way to meet the Almighty. The war made me question that belief. I saw decomposing human remains become food for scavenging animals and ravenous birds. At first I couldn't see how those people would meet God. It helped me to remember some Bible verses. "And the Lord God formed man of the dust of the ground and breathed into his nostrils the breath of life, and man became a living soul," and "In the sweat of thy face shalt thou eat bread, till thou return unto the ground; for out of it wast thou taken: for dust thou art, and unto dust shalt thou return" (Genesis 2:7 and 3:19). I came to realize that the spirit went to heaven, and the body was merely a vessel.

And when the misery around me made me wonder where God was, I remembered learning in Sunday school the story of how the Israelites escaped Egypt unharmed because God parted the Red Sea for them.

They had escaped the pharaoh's army, just as we had escaped the war. We were the remnants — the survivors — and God was with us.

Because Elijah and I had been staying with our maternal grandparents when the war broke out, I had no hope that our parents, if they had survived, would find us, not in a refugee camp in Tanzania. My grandparents were another matter, and I rekindled my hope of seeing them again. Once Elijah and I were settled in the children's tent, and I'd had the chance to recover from our exhausting journey, I began asking people about Gramma Kasine. I believed she was so well-known in our village that someone in the camp would be able to tell me if she were still alive. Looking back, I realize I was a bit too optimistic. In the end, no one I talked to knew or had heard of her. Kasine was also a fairly common name, so even if I found someone who knew a Kasine, it might not have been her. Not getting the answer I hoped for deeply disappointed me.

I knew that if Gramma were in the camp, she would have helped many people. I told myself that wherever she was, dead or alive, God was watching over her. In every situation, I heard her voice singing her favourite song, an impromptu melody with lyrics about the loving nature of the right breast. It brought me so much comfort as the days became weeks and then months. I sang the song while sitting and while walking. Soon, another song that was widely sung around the camp took its place:

What is being a refugee? Losing your people

And everything that

belongs to you and

falling into a stumbling block.

After about five months, we started going to the school under a tree. Most of us sat on leaves. The luckiest students sat on stones, which were more comfortable than the itchy grass. The teachers had no books, but they could read and write. They taught us how to sing and count in Swahili, the language in Tanzania, and Kinyarwanda. If the teacher singled you out to sing and you couldn't think of a song, the person sitting next to you would have to sing. I learned songs from different children, songs about their harsh lives, their parents and relatives, and the loving communities they once knew.

I loved to sing, and I had a song burning in my heart that I wanted to share, but I couldn't sing fluently in Kinyarwanda, and I wanted to wait until I was perfect. It was a song for my paternal aunt Karuhanga, whom I knew I would never see again. I wished my mother, grandmother, and Aunt Karuhanga were with me. There is a saying in Kinyarwanda, "Akabura nikaboneke ni nyina w'umuntu" — "The only thing that can be lost and never reclaimed is your mother." I know now, of course, that anyone can be a mother and take on a mothering role, but as a child in the refugee camp, I felt that my mother was lost to me forever and could not be replaced.

Sometimes I saw lucky children reunited with their families. Only a few were claimed by both of their parents. For most, only a mother or a father survived, and so the reunion also meant confirmation that one of their parents had been killed in the war. Other children learned from former neighbours that their parents would never come for them. I couldn't help fearing that someone I'd known would suddenly appear before me and break the news that my grandparents and other relatives had not survived.

There was little to do in the camp, so I started helping people too sick, weak, or injured to do things like gather firewood. Most evenings, with Elijah in tow, I would do acts of kindness, such as washing people's clothes, watching their pots to make sure they didn't burn while they took a nap, or collecting firewood. One evening, we came across an old woman lying under a blanket. When I sat beside her, I could tell that she was starving. Her bones protruded from her skin, and she was yawning in a way that indicated she was very lethargic.

"Where are your parents?" she asked.

"I don't have any parents," I replied.

"Is this your sibling?"

"Yes, Mama."

"Who is taking care of you?"

"We are living in that blue tent with other kids without parents," I said, pointing. Then I asked her if she had anything to eat. She told me she didn't; she'd been given beans and corn, but she didn't have firewood or water to cook them with.

"I can't do anything by myself," she said. "I lost all of my children and grandchildren. I am the only one remaining in my entire family. I can't have kids anymore because I don't have a husband, and I am old. It's pointless to be here. I will never be able to help myself or kids like you who don't have parents."

The sun was hot, and she was thirsty.

"Can I take your jerrycan and get some water for you?" I asked. "I don't know how to cook, but I can get firewood and water. Maybe you can show me how to cook."

"You are such a nice kid," she said.

"I can see that you need help, and there is nobody else here to help you."

"I think maybe you can get water for drinking," she said, pointing at her white jerrycan. "You are an angel for me, baby. God sent you here to me. God bless you!"

I picked up the jerrycan and beckoned to Elijah to follow, but the old woman suggested that I could leave him with her while I fetched the water. At first I agreed, but after taking a few steps, I suddenly felt that it was a bad idea to leave Elijah with a stranger. I turned around.

"It's boring to go alone," I said to the old woman. "I would like to go with my brother." We started walking. I had never been to the swamp before, but we met others we could follow. We walked for about fifteen minutes before reaching the swamp.

When we arrived, I saw people go into the swamp and get water, but I was so scared that I froze at the edge. The swamp near our home had saved me and Elijah, but it also almost killed us, and I had seen many people drown in big water like this. People would step onto grass not knowing there was water below. It was very scary to see people who were surviving in a war zone die in the simple act of stepping on the wrong place.

A woman asked if I needed help. When I said I did, she had me throw the jerrycan to her, and she filled it with water for me.

I trekked back toward the camp with the jerrycan on my head, Elijah trudging beside me. I tried to find the old woman, but the tents were close to each other and they all looked alike. I walked, walked, and walked with the full jerrycan on my head. I asked everyone if they had seen an old lady without a family, but they met my questions with blank stares. I searched all over for hours but could not locate the old lady's tent. Elijah began to cry. We were both tired and hungry and finally sat for a few minutes and drank some of the water in the jerrycan. Soon, night fell, and it was clear that we were lost. I had no idea how to find the orphans' tent. We lay down on the ground. I began to think about imigani, storytelling time at the fireplace with my paternal aunt. How I missed those moments. I started to tell Elijah the story of our escape. I told how I had heeded my intuition to take him with me to the swamp, saving his life. I was deep into my story before I discovered that he was fast asleep. It frightened me to think that if I had not taken him when I went to fetch the water, we'd have become separated. My intuition had helped me again. I lay beside him and slept too. In the middle of the night, I opened my eyes and saw God's love in the skies in the form of the moon and stars.

The next morning was sunny, but the morning dew made the air a little chilly. I woke up early because I wanted to avoid people who might ask questions about us. Elijah and I began to search for our tent. I knew it was a blue tent, but I could not find it. Again and again we asked people we met if they knew where to find the tent for children without parents. Finally, just as we were becoming exhausted, we met a woman who knew where the tent was and showed us how to get to it. My heart leaped for joy! I decided that after that, Elijah and I would stay close to the blue tent.

In the camp I met new people with their own stories. One rainy day I sat outside the tent watching a girl stirring fresh mud with a small stick. I asked her what she was doing.

"I am pretending to cook ugali," she said. People make ugali from any flour, like wheat, corn, or dried cassava. They boil water until it bubbles, then add the flour to the boiling pot and stir it until it's tender. It's cooked differently in different parts of Africa. "This is how my mother used to cook it," she explained, "and this wet mud looks like ugali."

I had tears in my eyes as I listened to the girl recall her mother's favourite dish, and so I waited patiently to see the girl's ugali out of respect for her mother's memory. Eventually, she put some of the mud in a leaf and then put water in another leaf.

"What is that?" I asked.

"We used to eat ugali and soup," she replied. She invited other kids nearby to eat. We sat in a circle, and she dipped her hand in the mud, took a piece, placed it in water, and started eating. The other kids started to laugh.

"You can't eat that!" I said to her. She vomited the mud all over the place.

A woman shared with us how she left her children in the forest. She had more than four of them, and they were toddlers. The father carried one while the mother carried another on her back, and the other two followed closely behind. The family was starving, and there was nothing to eat. The children cried without stopping. Finally, the desperate situation forced the husband to an unthinkable decision.

"We are going die with these crying babies," he said. "It is better to leave these kids and rescue ourselves."

"Then let me die with my kids!" the wife cried out. "You know very well that giving birth to them was a battle between life and death. I cannot imagine leaving my kids here. I would rather let them die in my arms. If we leave them here, I could not help but wonder if someone rescued them from danger. But if they died, I would see their dead bodies and know they are gone. There will be no room for regrets."

"Honey, do you remember when we met?" her husband asked. "Did you have any kids then? No? Then how did you get them?"

"Through you, of course."

"I have a tool that makes kids," he continued. "We shall make others. God knows we love them, but it's not wise to die here with them. You need to choose where you stand now."

What do you do if you are weak and Death is coming for you? What if you have three children, but you can't care for all of them? Do you let one child die to save the others? Do you let all the children die so you can live? The woman and her husband told their children to wait under a tree while they went in search of food. They walked away and never returned.

To this day, some children in Rwanda don't know that they were adopted by strangers who found them on the side of the road.

FOUR

The Long Journey

Elijah and I were playing a game with some other kids. We all sat in a circle, and then one of us would walk around with a cloth and sing, "Where is the baby cloth?" The rest of us would sing, "The cloth is just there going." The one with the cloth would put the cloth behind some-one in the circle. If you didn't realize that it was behind you, you would lose the game and have to sit inside the circle. If you knew they put it behind you, then you would pick it up quickly and run after the one who dropped it and try to throw it at their back. If you hit them, they would have to sit in the middle. If they could sprint and sit before you could tag them with the cloth, then you would sit back down in the circle.

We had been living in the camp for around eight months, and my hope that I would ever see my grandparents or parents again had almost vanished. Every day, the Red Cross posted a list of names of parents who were looking for their children. I didn't know how to read, so if no one from the Red Cross read the list aloud, I would ask someone to read the names on the notice board for me. Every day brought new disappointment for me.

As we were enjoying our game, someone told us that the Red Cross had just posted that day's list. The game stopped immediately and everyone ran. The other kids screamed and shouted as they jostled each other to get closer to the person reading the names. Anticipating that

Elijah and I would be disappointed yet again, I held back. The chaotic scene gradually calmed down, and the Red Cross worker started reading.

In alphabetical order, she called the first, second, and third names of parents and also the names of their children and the village where they were living. I paid rapt attention. I knew my chances were slim, but if I missed hearing the names of my family, she wouldn't read them again. I waited patiently for the letter *K*, the first letter in my grandmother's name. But my gramma's name was not on the list, and the woman kept reading through the *L*'s and *M*'s. Suddenly, I heard the name Nkuranga, and then my mother's name, and then Bosco's!

I jumped up and pushed through the noisy crowd. I threw my arms around the Red Cross worker and cried like a baby. Through my tears, I blurted out questions. "How did you find my family? Is everyone okay? Where are they now? Are they at home or with Aunt Karuhanga? Is it possible to see them today?" I tried to hug the worker again but, mindful of the rash on my skin, she didn't let me. She wrote down my information to forward to Uganda, where my mother and Bosco were, so that my parents would know where to find me and Elijah.

The news that my parents would find us was an enormous relief, but it was also bittersweet. Because the list had not included my grandparents' names, I took that to mean they were either missing or dead. Even so, I couldn't contain my excitement. I asked anyone wearing a Red Cross T-shirt when I would meet my parents. They always just told me to be ready, so from then on, I dressed carefully each day and carried a plastic bag with our belongings, such as our clothes, everywhere I went. I didn't want my parents to come and find me unprepared. When two weeks had passed and no one had come for us, I became convinced that no one ever would. I waited, and waited, and waited. Nothing happened.

One evening, while I sat weaving a bag that I planned to use if I one day attended a proper school, I looked up and saw a young man walking toward me. I didn't recognize him. He was sixteen or seventeen years old and wore an oversized jacket and short blue pants. He didn't seem to know me either. But then I looked closer and realized that this was the beautiful face of Bosco, my brother!

I jumped up and ran toward him. A look of uncertainty spread across his face. He was looking for a little girl and a small boy, and of course I had changed in the long months in the camp, and I was dressed like a boy. I grabbed him and hugged him like I would never let him go. "How is Mama?" I asked and quickly told him Mama's name. I felt the shock of recognition pass through his body when he realized he had found his sister.

Bosco grabbed my hand and Elijah's, and we made our way to a rock behind the tent, close to our playground, where we could sit and talk. Bosco's dry lips and dusty shoes identified him as an exhausted traveller. He had trekked a long, long way and had nothing with him, but he brought us hope.

"Where are Gramma and Grampa?" he asked.

"I can't tell you anything," I replied. "When the killers attacked us, I fled with Elijah. Then we found our way out of there. I have no idea if they are dead or not. Tell me, how did you find this camp? Is everyone okay?"

Bosco told me that everyone was fine and that they were staying with Nshwenkazi, one of our paternal aunts. He explained that they gave their names to the Red Cross, and eventually the Red Cross returned with our names and told them we were in a refugee camp in Tanzania.

"And you believed them?" I asked.

"Yes. There are many people who found their families through the Red Cross. I was very excited when I heard that you were in this camp and that Elijah was with you. I decided to come for you, but I got lost in the jungle. After three days of wandering, I went back. My next attempt was much easier because I came with a guide." The guide, Bosco said, had helped a lot of people. "There is a group of people returning to Uganda in three days, and we have to go with them."

"Do you mean I will spend another three days without seeing Mama?" I asked. He laughed. "I need to rest and get ready for the journey! Is it far?"

The journey from the camp in Tanzania to Uganda would take more than twenty-four hours of walking, and Bosco said he didn't know if Elijah and I would be able to make it. I, who would have been around nine years old, probably weighed less than thirty pounds. Given how underfed and sickly I looked, Bosco was especially worried about me, and he asked whether I had been given medication.

"A few days ago, a nurse gave me some, and I feel better now," I said. "Some of the rashes are drying up except for the ones between my fingers, which are very itchy. I struggle to eat, especially if the food is hot. I must wait until it is cold."

"Let's go and see the man who brought me here," he said. "We'll see what he says."

I wanted to get some clothes from the tent, but he told me to leave them behind for now. He expressed doubt that I'd be able to bring them on the journey because he would be carrying Elijah on his shoulders and wouldn't be able to help me carry them. "Let's go and see this man, and maybe we can come back for some items."

We walked in the chilly breeze that announced the arrival of sunset. The guide lived in a small hut covered with blankets and plastic sheets about fifteen minutes from where we lived in the camp. As we approached, we heard whispers from inside the hut that silenced as our footsteps became louder. People were always fearful that soldiers would attack at night, and I later learned that rebels attacked refugee camps in Tanzania and Uganda, killing people by the thousands. Five months after we left, Kagenyi, the camp that had protected us, was attacked and destroyed.

The guide was lying down outside with his eyes closed and his hands folded across his chest. He was exhausted.

"He is fast asleep," Bosco whispered. "Don't wake him." We sat outside, where the neighbours kept peeking at us through the torn blankets at their windows. The guide opened his eyes and looked at us. "These are your little brothers?" he asked Bosco. I wondered if Bosco would tell the guide that I was his sister.

"Yes," Bosco replied. To this day, he has never brought up the fact that when he found me in the refugee camp, I was passing as a boy. I don't know if he figured out for himself why I did it; in our culture no one ever talked about rape or the fears of girls.

"It is a miracle to see them alive," the guide said. "Do you think you will be able to travel with them?"

"I am not sure," Bosco said. "As you know, the journey is long, and I doubt if they can make it with how sick and weak they look. It will take God's help."

As I listened to them, I thought of everything Elijah and I had endured, and I told myself that even if I died at that moment, seeing Bosco again was enough. He could take Elijah back to Uganda, and one day Elijah could share the story of our struggle, although I wasn't sure how much of it he would be able to recall.

We spent that night with the guide's family. At dinner, they gave us corn mixed with black beans. After eating the same camp food for so many months, I had lost my sense of taste for good food. Even the memory of my favourite meal, mashed matooke with peanut sauce, was gone. I was famished, and yet I did not want to eat. My heart was so full of joy that I didn't care about my empty belly. I forced myself to eat at least some of the corn and black beans, knowing that I would need my strength for the journey ahead.

We stayed with the guide and his family for two days. There were around twelve people in his family, and most of them were grown up. On the third day, we were ready to start the journey. I asked Bosco if I could return to the orphans' tent to pick up the plastic bag that held my clothes, but he said no. The clothes themselves were not important to me, but I really wanted to say goodbye to the friends I would be leaving behind. Bosco wouldn't allow me to leave his side. He was worried I would get lost in the huge crowd in the camp, and he wanted to make sure we were close by and ready to leave when the guide said it was time. I didn't argue. I'd been looking after Elijah and making decisions for myself for months and my young mind was worn out. It was a relief to let Bosco take charge. I knew he would get us to our parents.

The sounds of whispers and quiet footsteps woke me. I sat up in fright, thinking that the camp was under attack. It must have been around four o'clock in the morning.

"Wake up!" Bosco said. "Other people are waiting for us outside."

"What's going on? Is anything wrong?"

"Everything is fine," Bosco replied. "Have you forgotten that we are going to Uganda?"

We'd leave as soon as it was light. It might seem that travelling under the cover of darkness would be the safer option, especially when the moon was bright enough to light our path. But travelling at night, even in the moonlight, is very scary. You don't know who you will run into, and since everyone is suspect during the night, simply walking down a road can make you seem like a thief. Should something happen to you, fewer people are around to help you. Travellers had been followed and lynched in recent months, particularly those whose inability to speak Swahili marked them as non-Tanzanian.

I shivered the whole time we waited. Ten of us were travelling: Elijah, myself, and eight adults. We travelled in three groups, pretending not to be together to avoid attracting attention. Bosco, Elijah, and I stayed together.

We walked and walked. It was inzira ndende, the long journey. After about six hours, my legs began to shake. Hunger made me want to vomit. I had never imagined I would have to travel such a long way again. But this time, I did not have to worry about Elijah, who rode on Bosco's shoulders, and I could tell Bosco about my discomfort. It also helped to know that I was walking to my parents.

We scrambled over rocks, crossed valleys, and climbed mountains through blistering heat and torrential downpours. One by one, my toenails fell off.

Two hills I will never forget: Mucucu and Rwabunuka. They loomed over me, and each time I thought, I am not going to be able to climb this mountain. I wondered if I could continue at all. People had been carrying bins of possessions and supplies, and when they saw the ascent, they started dropping them. I remembered crossing mountains on the way to Tanzania and felt overwhelmed and traumatized again. Thick bushes framed the dirt path that led up Mucucu. The path was clear, but it was not safe to deviate from it. Travellers had only recently created it, so the path was not wide. Two people could barely pass one another.

My shoeless feet and tired legs felt like stone. None of my body parts felt like they belonged to me. I doubted that I had the strength to climb. Forget about dying tomorrow instead of today, I thought, I would rather die now than climb this hill.

And then, instead of giving in to the physical agony, I listened to my mind. Something deep within told me it would be worth it to keep going, that each step forward would give me a strength I never knew existed, that I could find the hope of seeing my family again in the act of plodding on, one foot after the other. If I kept walking, I could tell them my story.

I made it up Mucucu, but my strength and courage deserted me when we reached Rwabunuka Hill. Mucucu had seemed impossible to me, and now I was facing a mountain that, I later learned, is 1,744 metres high. I told Bosco I could not do it: I would either return to the refugee camp or die on the spot. "My goal is to take you home, dead or alive," Bosco said, sweat dripping from his dirt-smudged forehead. He knew that if we died and our mother didn't see our bodies, she would not be able to rest. "Maybe they have even gathered to conduct a burial ceremony for all of us."

As he spoke, a woman passing by stopped. "Where are you coming from, and where are you going?" she asked. We had not eaten in at least eight hours, and I wanted to ask the woman if she had any food to spare, but Bosco gave me an intense stare that told me to keep my mouth shut and let him deal with her. We'd heard rumours of cannibals in the area. We were also fearful of being picked up the police or killed by locals because we didn't speak their language.

Bosco asked the woman which route was the best to take. We were separated from the guide and the others in our party, and Bosco had no map. Finally, I couldn't bear it any longer. "Can you please give me some food?" I begged. "I feel like I can't move my legs anymore. Please help me."

A glint of understanding flashed in her eyes and compassion softened her features. She understood my plea. She suddenly began to speak in Kinyarwanda.

"How did you know we speak Kinyarwanda?" Bosco asked.

"Ahh, I can tell you look like Rwandans," she replied. "Most Rwandans are brown. And besides, my grandparents are from Rwanda."

Bosco, anxious not to reveal too much about us, told her that we were actually Ugandan but could speak Kinyarwanda because we had family in both countries. The woman invited us to follow her to her house so she could see if she had something for us to eat.

Her kids were playing outside the house. She showed us where to sit outside. She apologized for not having any food ready, but she gathered some sweet potatoes and said she would cook them. I was so exhausted that I fell asleep on the ground. Bosco had to wake me up when the potatoes were ready. I had not tasted sweet potato in a very long time, and these did not taste the way I remembered my mother cooking them. She always cooked them with the skin on, so they tasted starchy rather than sweet. But that sweet meal was a lifesaver, and I was grateful. After we ate, the woman gave us some water, and then we returned to the hill. We were now quite far from the rest of our party.

It grew dark, and we had no idea where to sleep. Before the war, it was acceptable and common to knock on a stranger's door at night and ask for a place to sleep, but we no longer felt safe doing that. We'd seen what people did to one another. We decided to sleep in the forest. I thought it would be better to be devoured by wild animals than to suffer harm at the hands of fellow humans. We spotted a giant tree surrounded with tall grass, and Bosco suggested that we spend the night there. "It looks safe," he said. "It's far away from people's houses."

We gathered handfuls of grass to lie on and soon fell deeply asleep. During the night, an eerie sound woke me. At first, I thought something or someone was haunting us. As I strained my ears, I heard the sound again and breathed a sigh of relief. A distant thunderstorm was getting close enough to drown out Bosco's loud snoring. I fell asleep again, only to awaken when I heard the meowing of a cat. In my culture, when a cat cries, a person will soon die. Terrified, I woke up Bosco.

"Can you hear that?" I asked.

"What's that?"

"A crying cat," I said. "Maybe someone is planning to kill us!"

"Stop talking," Bosco said. "If someone hears you, you may bring a problem right to us!"

I couldn't get back to sleep. I lay shivering, and I prayed to touch Mama again. A heavy rain started to fall. As I had so many times before, I wondered why people had to suffer, especially children like me and Elijah. Hadn't we endured enough pain?

The rain fell and fell. It pooled on the ground and soaked the grass. Our grass beds began to float on the water, and we gave up trying to sleep. When morning finally came and we resumed our journey, we did so in soaked clothes. Eventually, the warmth of our bodies dried our garments.

Bosco and I agreed that we would walk for two hours and then rest for two hours. This would prolong our journey, but I knew I couldn't keep going without more rest time. Usually I slept on the ground while Elijah curled up on Bosco.

More than once I asked Bosco when we would reach our destination. He could not tell me. The other people and the guide had walked faster than us even before we stopped for our meal of sweet potatoes, and we were too far behind to be able to follow them. We spent days trying to figure out the route by asking strangers we met along the way. It was a dangerous way to map out a route. Before the war, it was common in Africa to stop a stranger and engage in conversation with them. But after the killings, it was hard to know whom to trust. Sometimes, we could tell a stranger was trustworthy by how they looked or the friendly way they spoke to us. Our appearances aroused curiosity. My bare swollen feet, bloated belly, and wounds attracted attention. Bosco found me a stick that I could lean on to help me walk. Finally, after what seemed an eternity of sleeping in thick bushes and asking strangers for food, I heard the words I'd been longing to hear.

"We are at the border!" Bosco shouted. We were at Kikagati, a crossing point between Tanzania and Uganda.

Bosco was familiar with the border because he used to go there to sell cows with Aunt Kurahanga's husband. Stepping onto the land of my ancestors and speaking Runyankore, my first language, I felt safe for the first time in months, and I immediately began to think about the family reunion to come. How would I greet Mama? Would she be excited to see me? What about Aunt Karuhanga or my cousins Fiona and Betesi? I knew I looked very different to the beautiful little eight-year-old who left Mama to visit her maternal grandparents, but I was confident that my family would welcome me as I was.

I knew many questions were waiting for me. Where would I start? What would I tell my mama about Gramma and how Elijah and I became separated from our grandparents? I was certain Gramma had died, and I was not ready to face that pain. I had often thought that I wanted my family to know my story, but now I decided that I would try to avoid answering whatever questions I could. A deep instinct told me that this was the way I'd find healing.

Thoughts of my family filled my head through the last leg of our journey and fuelled me to keep pushing forward. With each painful, exhausted step, I pictured myself seeing their faces and holding their hands once again. When we crossed the river, Bosco started assuring me that we were almost there. I wondered how I would hold my aunt when I saw her. I had no expectation that she would be the first person I would see. Excitement built in my heart even as I knew that I would have to hold stories back from her. My heart swirled with conflicting emotions and my mind filled with a jumble of thoughts. I was surprised that we were returning home safely and wondered how I, so dirty and dishevelled, would be received.

When we left the camp, we were mainly surrounded by Kihaya, the language spoken by the Tanzanians who lived near the camp. Now, as we got closer to my aunt's, I heard people greeting each other and speaking in Runyankore. I started to feel safer because I could express myself, talk to people, ask for food in my mother tongue. Language is a security blanket. It is connection, it is common understanding, it is being welcomed — it is everything.

We passed a matooke plantation filled with towering banana trees, which I never saw in Tanzania. It was a fresh and green reminder that I was making my way home. When my aunt's district, Ntungamo, came into view, the cows, the goats, the people fetching water and working on the plantations that had been so familiar to me were suddenly part of my life again.

FIVE

Finding My Aunt and Mama

In the front yard, my cousins and the neighbour's children were throwing balls made of banana fibres and giggling while they played. Aunt Karuhanga sat in front of the door, cheering. No one paid attention to the skinny child in tattered, filthy shorts and shirt. I felt like a stranger. Only when Bosco, who was a few steps behind me, came into view, Elijah on his shoulders, did the game stop.

Everyone ran to Bosco, hugging him and telling him how much they had missed him. And then their eyes settled on me. "Is that Kadur?" they asked.

Nobody could believe it was me. Aunt Karuhanga took me on her lap and her eyes flooded with tears. She touched every part of my body, taking in my wounds and rashes. She had never seen skin so damaged. Her children tried to console her, and they pleaded with her to stop crying, but she cried all the more.

"Please, let me cry," she said. "I'm so happy to see my kids again. You have no idea how my heart feels at this moment."

My cousins held on to Elijah as if they had just laid their hands on a lost pearl. Although he rode on Bosco's shoulders, he was as exhausted and dirty as I was. His crumpled clothing hung from his tiny frame. Bosco was also incredibly tired. A journey that might have taken around twenty-four hours to walk had taken us something like ten days, and Bosco had already made that long walk once.

While Aunt Karuhanga sobbed, I looked into her eyes. I wanted to cry, but all my tears were gone.

"Where is my mama?" I asked. "Where is my papa? What about my other siblings? Have you seen them?"

"My daughter, relax," she said. "I will tell you about your parents later. They are safe. They know you are with me."

Of course they couldn't have known, but I didn't question what my aunt said. She lied to calm me, and it worked. She promised that she would tell me about my parents in the morning. Then she instructed my cousin Fiona to heat water so I could take a bath. I asked Aunt Karuhanga if I could eat before I took a bath, but she smiled and said, "Bath first." She asked me what I would like to eat, and I told her I would happily eat anything.

When my aunt bathed me the rashes on my skin began to bleed and sting, making me cry. She assured me that the bleeding would hasten the healing. Afterward, she applied cow butter to my skin and wrapped me in a kitenge. She did the same for Elijah. Like Bosco, she never commented on the fact that I had come home dressed in boys' clothes.

She prepared matooke, my favourite dish, and served it with tomatoes, a pinch of salt, and a cup of milk. It was my first proper meal in months. My aunt warned me to eat in small bites or it would make me sick.

The following morning, enjoying the coziness of lying under a warm blanket in a room with an actual roof, I was the last person to get up. Word of our return had spread through the village, and I woke to the voices of many guests who had decided to join the elaborate party my aunt hosted in our honour. Villagers danced, ate, drank, and thanked God for keeping us safe. Although many struggled to recognize us as the children they'd once known, they were happy to see us. I could do nothing but sit and watch the celebration. I was exhausted, and I had a bad feeling in the pit of my stomach. Despite her promise, my aunt had said nothing about my parents, and I could not help wondering why, if they knew that Elijah and I were with Aunt Karuhanga, they did not come to see us. I began to think that they had died in the war.

That evening, after all the guests had gone home, my aunt started shaving my hair because it was so dirty and matted. Fearing what I might hear, I summoned all my courage. "Aunt, please be honest and tell me the truth. What happened to my parents?"

She told me that when the killing started, my parents and siblings made their way from Rwanda to Aunt Karuhanga in Uganda and lived with her for some months. My parents hoped the killings would end soon so they could go home, but the killings increased, and many Rwandans sought refuge in Uganda. Someone told them about a Rwandan refugee camp in Oruchinga. Bosco travelled there, hoping to find me and Elijah. No one could find our names in the UNHCR or Red Cross records, so he left his information with the Red Cross and, on their advice, began visiting other refugee camps. He returned to Aunt Karuhanga with the sad news that he couldn't find us anywhere. Then someone told him he should keep returning to Oruchinga, and so the next day he packed a small bag and left again.

"We were anxious about him because he never returned," my aunt said, "and we thought he had died on the journey or maybe someone had killed him. We had no clue that he had gone to Tanzania to get you and Elijah."

My mother stopped eating and sleeping once Bosco left, believing that she had lost three children to the war, including both of her sons. My father, my aunt said, had gone to stay with a cousin in Kantarama, about two hours away by foot. The longer Bosco's absence, the more my mother despaired. "Everyone had to keep an eye on her, because she once attempted to kill herself in the forest. Sometimes, at night, she would suddenly wake up and tiptoe to the door. We never allowed her to escape for fear that she might harm herself. We all stopped sleeping."

When she met someone who had just come from Oruchinga Camp, my mother decided to take my siblings and travel to the camp herself.

"She was bent on going with her remaining kids even though I pleaded with her to leave them with me." Fearful that my mother might harm herself on the way to the camp, Aunt Karuhanga decided to make the trip with her.

She and my mother packed a small bag, and with my siblings they hopped into a taxi that was heading to Oruchinga. At a marketplace called Kajaho Trading Centre people advised them to visit the UNHCR office in the Rwamurunga area, about a five-minute drive away. They arrived at the UNHCR office in the camp, which was about nine square kilometres in size and composed of around sixteen villages, just as they closed for the day. Aunt Karuhanga had only enough money for taxi fare to get home, so paying for lodging was out of the question. Refugees waiting for the office to reopen were sleeping on the ground — men, women, elders, and kids. My aunt, mother, and siblings spent an unpleasant night sleeping under a tree.

In the morning, the UNHCR served porridge to the refugees, including my family, and then began registering people. My family waited under the tree for their turn. When my mother reached the registration desk, they asked her many questions.

"How many kids do you have?"

"I have three now, but I had six altogether."

"Where are the other three?

"I believe they are dead."

"Are you not sure if they are dead?"

"Two of them were with my mother in Rwanda before the war. I don't know if they are still alive, because I have not heard any news from them. I came here to see if they are here."

"By God's grace, you may find them here. We have many kids without parents. For some of them, we have received confirmation of the death of their parents. The Red Cross is still searching for the remaining orphans' families in other refugee camps in Africa. If you tell us their names, we can search our records to see if they are here."

My mother explained that Bosco had come to the camp to search for me and Elijah, and the officer told her he would see if the camp had a record of Bosco. He went away and another worker completed the process, asking about my father's whereabouts and whether or not he planned to reunite with our family. Then the first man came back. He told my mother that her children were in Tanzania, in Kagenyi Camp, and that Bosco had gone to find us.

"Your mother jumped up in excitement after hearing the news," my aunt said. "She was soon on her knees, praising God for saving her children. The people surrounding us thought she had lost her mind. I was so joyful, but I knew it was not over until we saw you in the flesh."

The UNHCR gave them plastic sheeting for a tent, blankets, and some cutlery and dishes and assigned them a place in the camp where they could build a tent. The tent would barely keep the rain off them and was too small for five people: my mother and aunt had to crawl through the opening, and once inside they could only lie flat. My aunt, who had Ugandan citizenship and a home, knew she couldn't bear it. The next day, she left the camp and returned to her own children. My mother and siblings remained because they were Rwandan and therefore not free to live in Uganda for long periods of time. I think she also hoped that being in the camp would make it easier for people to help her locate me and Elijah and bring us back to her if we were still alive.

Listening to my aunt, I thought about the suffering that Elijah and I had endured in our months away — so much worse than a night in a crowded, low-roofed tent! — and what it had taken for Bosco to lead us home. As I learned from my aunt that day, Bosco's quest to find us had been much more prolonged and difficult than he'd said. After he'd returned to Oruchinga, he registered as a refugee so that he could get food, water, shelter, and clothing, just as my mother would. He'd been in the camp for a month when the Red Cross finally told him that Elijah and I had been found in Tanzania and how to reach the camp. He set off on his own, got lost, and found his way back to the camp. This time he met the guide who was leading other refugees to Kagenyi to find their relatives, and Bosco travelled with them. And then, after all that, he brought Elijah and me home. Bosco risked his life to walk over land and across borders, the threat of ethnic violence always near, to rescue us because he loved and valued us. He was a hero.

After one week recovering with Aunt Karuhanga, Bosco and I decided to take Elijah and go to Oruchinga to find our mother and siblings. My cousins didn't want me to go, but I promised that I would be back once I found Mama. We wouldn't need to walk: Aunt Karuhanga gave us taxi fare, and early one Thursday morning we left.

It was market day, and if we showed up late at the car park, we would miss all the taxis. After traversing hundreds of kilometres on foot, I thought the only vehicles that existed were the ones belonging to the Red Cross and UNHCR. The prospect of travelling in a minibus to Oruchinga was a luxury to me.

As we waited for the minibus to fill with passengers, I spotted a seller hawking traditional doughnuts. My father had once bought some of these doughnuts for me, and I knew they were a favourite of my mother. I wanted to get some for her. I asked Bosco if we had any extra money, but he wanted to make sure he had enough to pay our fares. "They might charge extra money," he told me, "and if you don't pay, they can bite you. I don't want any trouble with these men."

Travelling by bus in Uganda is a risky business. Minibuses are typically built for fourteen people, but the drivers want to make as much as money as possible, so they overload them. The roads are usually dirt and marked with axel-breaking potholes. Many accidents result from vehicles passing each other on roads meant for only one. No one uses seatbelts, so when accidents happen, the passengers fly everywhere, and many die. Many drivers have fake licences. Some haven't even passed a driving test. If they get caught, a bribe to the police is enough for the bus to continue on its way. We were travelling in a minibus stuffed with twenty-four passengers. Almost every passenger carried an extra person on their lap. Elijah sat on Bosco, and I had to sit on the lap of a young woman. Even the driver shared his seat with another person!

The minibus left for the camp at about nine o'clock. The embankment separating the road from the Kagera River was not wide, and I was sure the bus would fall into the river. Fortunately, our driver navigated the road with great skill. Forty minutes into the journey, I told Bosco that I needed to pee. Bosco spoke to the driver, but the driver said he couldn't stop. I tried hard to hold it, but I became so uncomfortable that I asked Bosco to speak to the driver again.

"I told you, I can't stop!" the driver barked. "If you leave this car, that's the end. I will still get my full money for the trip."

Some passengers pleaded on my behalf, but it fell on deaf ears. I began to sob with desperation. Other passengers pleaded with me to stop crying; perhaps they feared the driver would get so angry with me that he would leave me at the side of the road. I crossed my legs as tightly as I could. Finally, we reached Kajaho Trading Centre, and the driver pulled over. When I stepped out of the bus, I couldn't hold it for even a second longer. I just squatted in front of the minibus and urinated on the ground. Everyone stared at me, but I didn't care.

We had only a short walk to reach a camp that looked very much like the one where Elijah and I had lived: blue and green tents with plastic sheets for extra rain protection. We started asking people where to look for Mama and were told she would probably be in the Kazinga zone, an area designated for newcomers. The camp was so big and so crowded that the walk took us an hour and a half.

In the Kazinga zone we found a small market full of people selling various items and food like matooke, bananas, and cassava. We approached a woman and asked if she had seen a woman with two daughters and a son. "There are many women with three kids," she replied. "It's hard to know which one you are looking for. Can you tell me what your mama looks like?"

"She is a brown lady," Bosco said. "She is of average height and doesn't usually cover her head. She has a black birthmark on her right eye."

"I think I know that lady," a man standing nearby said. "She stays in one of those tents over there." He pointed to a cluster of tents a few hundred metres away and offered to walk over with us. He led us to a tent where a woman was facing away from us, sitting on a stool, preparing beans to cook.

"Good afternoon," the man said. When she didn't answer, the man moved closer, catching her eye, and she turned her head. As soon as I saw her face, I knew. This was the face I had long dreamed of seeing and feared I never would. Without a second thought, I jumped on her. Startled, she pushed me away, but then she saw Bosco and Elijah. She hugged us to her and began to cry as though she would never stop.

"Is this you or someone else?" she asked me as she held my hands and studied my thin frame and damaged skin.

"Ah! It's hard to say," I said.

I was at a loss for words to explain what I had gone through. And although I was very happy, I didn't feel free to say so. Not only could I not find the words to tell Mama how scared I had been, but I felt I couldn't even cry. In our culture, we're not supposed to show our emotions. My mother has never said "I love you" to me. Parents express their love for their children by cooking for them or talking about what they've done for them. I've always thought that when you're happy, you should be able to laugh. When you're sad, you should be able to cry.

"Just take me the way I am," I told Mama. "I cannot tell you anything now, but the time will come when I will be able to tell you everything."

I had thought that once we found Mama and our siblings, we'd return to Aunt Karuhanga's, but I was mistaken. We had no status in Uganda and so weren't permitted to live with my aunt. Mama took us to the UNHCR reunification centre. They gave us clothing and a family food-ration card. Every two weeks we'd receive food Mama would cook for us. Because we spoke mainly Runyankore, some people in the camp questioned whether we were Rwandan. They thought maybe we were poor Ugandans who'd come to the camp just to get food and other stuff meant for refugees.

The Oruchinga Camp was much like the Kagenyi Camp in Tanzania with the exception that Oruchinga did not have as many sick and weak people. The food that the Red Cross provided was good, but the quantity did not feed our family. The food allotted for a month would be gone in a week and a half. We were always hungry and would try to earn money by working in people's gardens. We'd spend what we'd earned in the camp market, buying matooke and cassava.

We bathed outside in a shed made of grass where our neighbours could tell if we had spent days without bathing. The toilets were pit latrines with no privacy. We had no toilet paper, so you would wipe with leaves or sit on the ground and slide on the grass. The same flies that infested the latrines would buzz around the food we cooked and ate. No wonder diseases such as hepatitis-A spread quickly. The camp had functional schools for grades one to seven, but no medical facilities. Locals told us a hospital was a three-hour walk from the camp, and that is where we would go in an emergency. I would end up travelling to that hospital many times. We never had to pay for treatment, which was likely covered by humanitarian organizations. Because there were so many refugees, sometimes we would go to the hospital only to find that they had no medication to give us.

I became friends with a young Canadian woman named Chinook, a worker with Right to Play, a humanitarian organization that strives to help children living in impoverished and conflict-ridden nations. I can still see her in her yellow T-shirt with the Right to Play logo on the front. Chinook and her colleagues brought happiness and joy to the kids in the camp, and Chinook played with us and became part of us. She never made me feel like I was less than a human being just because I was a refugee. She always seemed to be holding a baby and would smile widely whenever an infant approached her.

We had been living in the camp for approximately six months when my father came. He brought with him his second wife, Dorosera, and their children. Dorosera had one son and three daughters from a previous relationship and one son and daughter with my father. Like us, my father and his second family had no status in Uganda, and the fierce fighting in Rwanda made it impossible for any of us to return. Bosco took Dorosera and her children to register as refugees. They were given their own tent to live in, and my father came and went as it suited him. For the foreseeable future, Oruchinga Camp would be our home.

One day, I went to fetch water. When I returned home, I saw someone outside our tent with my mother. The face was familiar, but I couldn't place it. When my mother helped me to remove the heavy jerrycan from my head and I wiped the sweat from my eyes, I realized that my grandmother Kasine was standing in front of me. For her part, she hadn't recognized me, either. I threw myself on her.

On that awful day when we fled, my grandparents had also managed to make their way to Tanzania. They were in a different refugee camp from the one where Elijah and I lived. Then, in 1996, the Tanzanian government demolished all the Rwandan refugee camps. Most refugees were forced to go back to Rwanda. They were beaten up by the police and some were killed on the way; many died before they made it.

Somehow, my grandparents got to Uganda and to Oruchinga Camp. They had no idea that we were in the camp, too. They lived in the Kafunzo zone for some weeks. We might never have found each other had not Bosco, who moved around the camp more than anybody else in our family, encountered them in the Kafunzo zone.

My extended family on my mother's side is much bigger than on my father's side and so was more widely impacted by the war. I know very little about what happened to my father's siblings. My mother's family was scattered across many camps in Tanzania. We would eventually piece their stories together and learn what had befallen them. Some didn't survive the war.

My grandmother and I had always had good conversations. I was able to be very open with her. I told her things I kept from my mother because my mother had her own troubles, and I didn't want to share my pain and make her cry. I thought that Gramma and I would talk about what we had been through. I wanted to know what had happened to her. But as the weeks passed, I realized that she didn't want me to know. We just pretended that we were all okay.

SIX

The Man Who Fought the Leopard

Life in the camp was difficult. It was a struggle to get enough food to feed all of us. My mother was responsible for serving the food, and she was fair to everyone. When she didn't have enough food, we'd sit in a big circle in the centre of the tent. My mother would pour the food in the middle of the circle; a layer of banana leaves kept the food from landing on the dirt. Then the eating competition would begin! The size of your hand determined how much food ended up in your belly. The smaller children usually left such dinners crying because they got only a bite before the food disappeared.

My father's arrival with Dorosera and their children also brought conflict and violence into our lives. I clenched my teeth when I watched Dorosera's children play with my father and call him Papa. He never beat them the way he beat his children with my mother, and his obvious preference for them sickened me. He was my father, too, and yet he made no effort to find me and Elijah. Even when Bosco told him that the Red Cross had located us in a refugee camp in Tanzania, my father had not brought us to Uganda. Instead, he chose to leave my mother and siblings, first to live with a cousin and then to join his second family. And when my father joined us in the camp, he never acknowledged Bosco's heroism.

Dorosera took advantage of her status as my father's preferred wife. She used any excuse to get my mother in trouble, knowing what would happen. She must have wanted my father all to herself, or maybe she just enjoyed watching my father beat my mother. All Dorosera had to say was "Your wife did this to me!" and my father would descend on my mother and beat her. Our neighbours soon gave up trying to stop the beatings. Nobody messed with him. Everyone feared and respected him as the man who fought a leopard and won, and the sad truth is that husbands commonly beat their wives and nobody says anything about it. She is his wife. She didn't marry him; *he* married *her*. I grew up hearing comments like that, but I never understood why it had to be that way. The plight of women in my culture always reminded me of the stories about slavery we heard around the fire. Slavery and the misogyny that surrounded me seemed much the same to me: people from other countries kidnapped Africans and shipped them overseas to toil in slavery, and in Africa we created slaves from our own women and made that practice a deeply entrenched cultural value.

Some neighbours in the camp brewed their own alcohol, and it became my father's favourite drink. When he drank, his behaviour worsened. Dorosera also liked to drink herself into a stupor. We grew used to him coming to the tent drunk, his clothes reeking of gin. If it were evening, we'd conceal ourselves under the blankets, pretending to be sick, or hide outside the tent. He would take whatever was cooking on the makeshift stove and pour the contents onto the ground. On those nights, we slept on empty stomachs. If we dared to complain, he'd strike us with a cane. Living with my father meant living in terror.

I will never forget the day he came home with a box of cookies, a gift from Frank, one of the Red Cross workers. Later, Dorosera sent one of her daughters, Mutesi, to steal the cookies from Papa's vault. His vault was just a basket beside his bed, but none of us would dare to even think about touching it. Because we lived in a tent, Dorosera's children came in any time they wanted, and my mother couldn't stop them. When

Papa returned in the evening, he searched everywhere — the pockets of clothes, inside saucepans, bags — but could not find his cookies.

"Kadur!" he shouted angrily. I was outside the tent, playing with other kids, but as soon as I heard his voice my heart started racing. I knew from experience that situations like this ended in a severe beating, even if I had done nothing wrong. He never listened to my pleas of innocence. My mother could have watched him in silence as he flogged me, but she often tried to defend me or pleaded with him to spare me, which meant that he would beat her, too.

He shouted my name a second time. "Yes, Papa!" I answered and went into the tent. He slapped me on the chin and ordered me to stay in the corner, and then he summoned Elijah into the tent as well.

"I left a box of biscuits here, and it's gone," he said to Elijah. "You and your sister were the ones at home, which means you ate them!"

We denied knowing anything about it, but he did not listen. He told us to wait for him and went out to get his bicycle chain. He had three tools he used to beat us with: the bicycle chain, slippers called umoja, and a leather belt. The slippers did the least damage. The leather belt meant you couldn't sit down for a week. A flogging with the bicycle chain would take you to the very gates of Hell. Only God could have saved you from the bicycle chain.

"Instead of dying here," I whispered to Elijah, "let's run, and save our death for another day." With that, we crawled out of the tent and fled. We stopped to see if our father was chasing us, but we saw no one. We slept in a tree that night. I thought about the thrashing my poor mother had surely suffered because of our disappearance.

In the morning, on her way to fetch water, one of our friends saw us in the tree. When she returned home, she told my father where she'd seen us. He got on his bicycle and rode to the tree, where Elijah and I were trying to figure out what to do next.

My father dropped his bicycle and ran toward us. There was no way we could outpace him, so I told Elijah not to run. For a second, I prayed for the ground to swallow me.

My father tied my hands with a stretchy rope and tethered me to the right side of his bicycle. He did the same to Elijah on the left side. Papa rode his bike like a warrior returning home with the spoils of war, flogging us the whole way. We stumbled and fell many times. No one intervened on our behalf. Rather, they encouraged him. "Kill them!" they shouted. "They are *your* kids!" And in our community, they were right. He had complete control of our lives. Like Mama, we belonged to him.

By the time we reached the tent, our hands were bleeding from where the rope had cut into our skin. When Mama saw us tethered to the bicycle, she hid in our neighbour's tent. She could not bear to witness the whipping that awaited us.

In the corner, I saw Dorosera giggling. I wished my father would just flog us to death, and if he didn't, I wished that I could run away from home. But I had nowhere to go. Aunt Karuhanga lived too far away, and I didn't want to leave my sweet mama. Why couldn't he choose his second wife and leave us in peace? More than once, I tried talking my mother into divorcing him, but she feared he would kill her. Even if she were bold enough to leave him, she'd become an outcast in our community, mocked and taunted.

There is a saying in Kinyarwandan, "Amafuti y'umugabo nibwo buryo bwe" — "A man's shots or decisions are his way, and inherently praiseworthy." It means that everything he does is right. If a woman filed for divorce and her parents were still alive, they would have to return to her spouse twice the amount they received for her dowry, a penalty that trapped many women in abusive marriages. If the parents received twenty cows for their daughter, they would have to return forty cows to the husband, and few families had the means to do that. The actual cows they'd received at the time of the marriage were either dead or had been traded for land. The social stigma of divorce meant that even if the parents could pay the penalty, they might still expel their daughter from their family home, and then where would she go? Divorce was almost never an option. You stayed with your husband and endured the pain. If you didn't talk about the abuse that you endured, people would call you a good and intelligent woman. Those who spoke out were labelled weak and stupid.

One morning, Eugenia, my half-sister, came to our tent. The day before, my father had given my mother a small amount of money, and Eugenia said that he had sent her to get it back. She carried with her one of his shirts as proof. That was something my father did: when he sent someone to fetch something, especially if it involved money, he would give them one of his shirts to prove that he had issued the order. My mother didn't hesitate. She gave Eugenia the money.

When my father came back to the tent that night, he asked for the money. He planned to go to the bar for a drink. "What money?" my mother asked. "I gave Eugenia the only money I had when you sent her over to get it."

"Are you stupid?" he bellowed. Knowing it would not go well for my mother, I crawled into our neighbour Daforoza's tent. I heard my mother screaming as my father beat her senseless. After several long minutes, my father left her lying on the ground. A crowd quickly gathered. Many believed my mother was dead. Daforoza checked and found that she was breathing but unable to speak.

The camp had no ambulances, so men would carry sick or injured people to the hospital in ingobyi. They would take turns carrying the patient, two in front and two behind, until they reached the hospital. About sixteen men showed up to carry my mother. I followed with a basin, some clothes, and a few things I knew my mother would need. Tears soaked my shirt.

My mother was in the hospital for three days, and I stayed with her. My father never came to see her. Our neighbours brought us food, and Gramma looked after my siblings. I tried to talk to my mother about leaving my father, but all she would say was, "You are still young. You think it's easy to leave, but it is not."

My father's behaviour was not unusual in our culture. Daforoza's husband, Rurinda, had two other wives. Our community considered him rich and treated him like a king, just like it did other men with multiple wives. Having more than one wife increased a man's ability to father children. Sons, of course, were best, but if a man had twenty girls from several wives, he might get two cows for each of them as dowry when they wed. Forty cows were a rich man's wealth.

Rurinda, like many men in our community, did nothing to help his wives. His only task was to decide which wife he wanted to sleep with on which days — and occasionally he would act as a marriage counsellor for other families. People believed that a man with many wives must be intelligent and that this qualified them to settle marriage and family disputes for others. Of course, Rurinda and men like him always advised wives to respect their husbands and never talk about what happened within the home. I promised myself I would never be any man's second wife, and if my husband married another, I would end our marriage. I would also forbid my husband from paying a dowry for me because I didn't want to be traded like a commodity or have my worth measured in the value of a cow.

Mama was terrified that my father would beat her again as soon as we returned to the tent. We knew no one would help. My maternal grandfather was perhaps the nicest person I knew, very quiet and loving. He loved his children, and he never treated Gramma the way my father treated my mother. But he was a product of our culture. He turned against Aunt Janet when those men raped her, and as much as he loved my mother, he never said a word about my father's abuse. My father paid him the dowry, and she was no longer his daughter. She belonged to my father.

I felt strongly that as long as the two families lived near each other and as long as Dorosera continued to manipulate my father, it would be only a matter of time until my father killed Mama. And then one day Mutesi and I were in a heated argument and she threatened to tell her mother on me. "Maybe you've forgotten about the last incident when we had your mother beaten," she said, and then she bragged about how her mother had sent Eugenia to get the money just so that my father would beat Mama. She actually laughed as she told me that my father had asked her mother and Eugenia if they'd taken his money and they denied it.

Daforoza overheard everything. She told my father, and he confronted Mutesi. She admitted to what had happened. He then did the unimaginable. He sent Dorosera and her children to live in another village in the camp, fifteen minutes away from our tent. Dorosera remained his favourite wife, however. I prayed that he would stay with his second family and never return. If that happened, at least we could sleep well.

Bosco was the firstborn, and he felt pressured to get married. There was nothing else to do, and everyone his age was getting married. No one wanted to die without experiencing the affection and physical pleasures of romantic love. That was especially true of girls, since sex before marriage was forbidden to them. Boys had no restrictions, and it was normal for them to have lots of sex before marriage. Bosco was handsome. His brown skin was so light that he could pass as white. People often called him Kazungu, meaning that he looked like a white man. Light skin was so prized that some people would spend what little money they had on skin-bleaching lotions like Caro Light or Caro White instead of purchasing food.

Bosco fell in love with a girl in the camp named Betty. Every evening, he went to Betty's tent and helped her parents. Betty had no idea Bosco was in love with her; she was only around fourteen, much younger than Bosco, and not ready for love or marriage. Bosco knew that if her parents said yes to his proposal, Betty couldn't refuse. He worked hard to please her parents. Betty rejected Bosco's marriage proposal, claiming she was in love with someone else and they had plans to marry soon, though this was a lie. Three days later, she became a victim of guterura: another man, someone she had never met but who also had his eye on her, sent hoodlums to kidnap Betty, and she was married by force to a stranger.

When Bosco found out about Betty's marriage, he was heartbroken. He became an angry man, and he openly lusted after anyone in a skirt. He turned his attention to a girl named Vestine. She was fifteen or sixteen years old and a smart fifth-grader (the war had interrupted her schooling, putting her behind her age group). Her father was one of the few parents that wanted his daughter to be educated, and she planned to finish high school. My brother found this attractive. But instead of trying to impress Vestine and her parents and risking rejection, as had happened with Betty, Bosco decided that he would have Vestine kidnapped. I knew of his plans because we slept near one another in the tent. I overhead him talking with the men he hired while I pretended to snore like a deep sleeper.

I wished that I could run to Vestine's house and warn her what was about to happen. I knew that if I dared open my mouth, all manner of punishment would rain down upon me. Fearing Bosco's wrath, I kept my mouth shut. I also knew that I couldn't have saved Vestine. Even if I had warned her, she wouldn't have been able to hide forever. If I had told her father of the plan, he could only have protected Vestine by staying by her side constantly, which would have been impossible. People would have shamed Vestine's father if he confronted Bosco. "Oh, are *you* going to marry her then?" they would have asked. Guterura was an accepted practice.

My sister Godance and I were with Vestine and her friends when she was kidnapped. We were on our way home from fetching firewood. Without warning, a group of young men emerged from where they'd been lying in wait and charged at us. We dropped our firewood and ran, but one of them, Kagenzi, caught Vestine and pushed her to the ground. They tied her hands and gagged her so she couldn't scream. Vestine's muffled cries for help were barely audible as Kagenzi carried her away across his shoulders like a hunter's game.

The kidnappers took Vestine to a small house that Bosco had secretly built. It had walls of grass and a thatched roof. Kagenzi and the others left Vestine and Bosco alone in the house and waited outside to see if Vestine would lose her virginity.

All through the night, Vestine refused to have sex with Bosco. When victims of guterura refused to submit and fought off their husband's advances, his friends would hold her down. This practice was called kumviriza, and the next morning the friends would tell stories about what had happened to the girl the night before. This is what happened to Vestine. Kagenzi entered the house to hold Vestine down for Bosco. Vestine finally gave up. She cried while Bosco's friends cheered him on, celebrating that he had finally become a man. At that moment, Vestine became Bosco's wife. To this day, my culture has no concept of marital rape.

When Vestine's father learned of his daughter's forced marriage, he was furious. He went to Bosco's house to take back his daughter. "I need my daughter!" he shouted. "You cannot just take my daughter like that. I only have girls, and I have plans to send them to school. My daughter is everything to me!"

A crowd soon gathered, and several people offered their unsolicited opinions.

"That's not right, Katabarwa. You can't take her back!"

"If you take your daughter back to educate her, who is going to marry her when everyone knows that she already had sex with a man?"

"Katabarwa, you are wasting your time. Your daughter is now a woman."

Everyone advised him to stop embarrassing his daughter and instead approach my parents for Vestine's dowry. The dowry should have been about two hundred dollars or the equivalent in goods or livestock, but my parents had no money and no possessions. They promised they would pay if their situation changed. Vestine's father died a couple of years later, so no money was ever exchanged.

A new bride goes through a transformation from girl to woman. Bosco had purchased slippers and some kitenge for Vestine. No longer could she have girls as friends or wear skirts like them. From this moment on, she would need to keep the company of married folks and wear her kitenge, indicating that she was a married woman. She also had to grow her hair long.

Vestine was required to stay in Bosco's makeshift house for three weeks during this transition while girls from the village came to visit. Although these traditional visits were supposedly about pampering the new bride and helping her to look beautiful, they really made it possible for girls to ask questions about the bride's sexual experience. It was their chance to hear about sex from a friend. With each passing day, the house teemed with girls eager to hear stories of how it felt to eat the forbidden fruit. Now I can only imagine Vestine's discomfort at entertaining these questions when my brother had forcibly subdued her and she felt no love for him.

Vestine was completely unprepared for the responsibilities that came with entering womanhood at such a young age and so violently and abruptly. She worried about the risk of childbirth and the difficulties of raising children, particularly in a refugee camp. The hospital was far enough away that women often had their babies en route. If a pregnant woman began delivering her baby on the way to the hospital, the men carrying her on an ingobyi would pull the baby out, hoping to save the child and the mother. Every pregnant woman travelled with sharp blades to cut the umbilical cord and thread to tie it. Quite apart from the pain and fear they endured, women who delivered babies this way were humiliated and embarrassed at having displayed their private parts in front of strange men.

My brother's actions were reprehensible to me, but he was a product of the extreme patriarchy of the culture we grew up in. Vestine's life with him illustrates the sad state of women's rights in Uganda. She was robbed of her bright future. She got pregnant within months of the marriage and has borne multiple children since then, none of whom have been able to pursue an education. Her relationship with Bosco was always fraught. Having learned from our father's example, he was never faithful to Vestine. He'd impregnate her, leave her for long periods, and then return to impregnate her again. The idea in our culture that women who stay with their husbands are brave and honourable endures and explains why Vestine refused for many years to leave Bosco. Only when Bosco contracted HIV and passed it to her did she cut ties with him. Now she is alone, looking after four children and vulnerable to getting even sicker from HIV because Uganda does not have the health care to help her manage her condition. She is frail, giving up money she needs for food to pay for whatever HIV medication she can afford. It's a tragedy.

Bosco, meanwhile, has been unable to make a home of his own. More than once over the years he's returned to live with our parents, and he continues to suffer at the hands of our violent father. A few years ago, my father beat Bosco so badly that he nearly died. I abhor what Bosco did to Vestine, but I cannot forget all the times he looked out for me and cared for me before the war, and nothing can change the love and gratitude I feel toward him for saving me and Elijah from the camp in Tanzania.

I ache for Vestine, and I ache for Bosco.

SEVEN

A Twig Strike in the Eye Sharpens Your Gaze

I began to feel the weight of responsibility on my shoulders, and I jumped in to help my mother care for my younger siblings. My life followed a numbing routine. I woke up at five and swept the floor of the tent for an hour. Then, with a nagging pain in my back, I took a forty-litre jerrycan and embarked on my first visit of the day to the swamp to fetch water. The round trip took thirty minutes. I would make the trip at least three times every day. I was scared that I might fall in and drown and often waited until someone arrived who could fetch the water for me. I always tried to use the big jerrycans to reduce the number of trips I had to make. With the large container sitting on my head, you could barely see me. The source of our drinking water was also where we went to bathe and wash our clothes. We had no means to boil our drinking water, and huge numbers of people died from drinking dirty water. Although my siblings sometimes helped, some of them had run away from home, desperate to escape our father's violence. Mama would get up early and go to work either in our small garden, where we grew our own beans and maize, or in other people's gardens to earn money for food. I was given the lion's share of responsibility in the house and was known as the family's most active girl.

Once, I told Mama that I would dig a hole for a toilet if it took me a month. "People will laugh at you," she said. "Girls do not do those things. They are for men and boys." If it's for men, I wondered, why hasn't my father done it? I started digging. After three days, neighbours came to help me. It took three weeks, but we had a toilet. Next, I started building a house for myself because our house wasn't big enough for all of us and everyone slept on the ground. The only thing people helped me with was putting on the roof, because I was a girl and not allowed to climb.

Constant chores and waiting at the well gave me time to think. I think I must have been around twelve years old by then. What will my future be like? I wondered. Is there a way out of this life? Who would marry me? Would getting married at this age help me? I felt trapped on a path I didn't choose.

I knew I wanted to help people. I wanted to be like Doreen, one of the Red Cross workers. I liked Doreen's life, or what I knew of it. She was a school worker. She loved playing with us, and she wasn't one of the ones who tried to avoid touching us. She never made me feel dirty or inhuman because of the situation I was in. I loved her fluffy ponytail, the fact that she always had shoes on her feet, and especially how men and women obeyed her instructions. Knowing the cultural importance of marriage to us, she taught us that true beauty lay in education. When you are educated, she said, you can get a good job, and then you can work on yourself and look so beautiful that every man who sees you will want to marry you. I wondered how Doreen had done it: had she attended the best schools at an early age? Did her parents encourage her and pay for her education? I thought I would like to help refugees heal from the scars of war. A proverb in Runyankole is, "Akati Ku kakuteera omu riisho Kati hweza" — "a twig strike in the eye sharpens your gaze." Because I knew what it felt like to be a refugee, I thought I could use my experience to help others. But I couldn't read or write. I would need an education.

I was poised to go to school before the war, but now that dream seemed out of reach. Education wasn't for girls like me who spent their days doing household chores and taking care of their younger siblings. I had loved what little schooling I received at the camp in Tanzania. But whenever I thought of going back to school, I felt that my situation was hopeless. No one in my family could read or write. And my attachment to my mother was powerful; I knew she needed me.

Shortly before sunrise one morning, Mutesi, who was around eight years old, woke up very ill and complaining of stomach pain. One of her siblings came to get me, and my father told me to take Mutesi to the hospital. None of her full siblings was willing to make such a long trip. She was too weak to walk, so I placed her on my back and began the long trek to the hospital. After two hours I tried to get her to walk, but she couldn't move her legs. She shivered and her skin felt cold while sweat poured off me. I had no choice but to put her on my back again.

The line for the clinic was so long that I wondered if we would ever see a doctor. The hospital staff had joined red benches together for the patients to use, so we sat on a bench and began the long wait. Some people ignored the line and walked right into the clinic. Nurses would also usher in people they knew ahead of all the people patiently waiting their turn. We sat and watched people eating bananas and African doughnuts while our bellies rumbled.

Finally, it was our turn. The nurse said Mutesi had a fever and that pinworms, contracted from drinking contaminated water, were causing the abdominal pain. Without proper toilets or wells, we had no way to avoid drinking tainted water in the camp. People, mostly children, were always getting sick and even dying from the unhygienic conditions. The nurse gave Mutesi some tablets wrapped in paper and advised us to boil our drinking water to make it safe. That was much easier said than done. Even if we could have found a way to boil it, we didn't have an extra jerrycan to hold it once boiled. And because we spent so much time outside, and it was so hot, we were always drinking water. Without water bottles we could just carry with us, we drank whatever water we could find.

Fortunately Mutesi felt much better after taking the medicine the nurse gave her. She was able to do some of the walk home on her own. When she got tired, we'd sit to rest or I would piggyback her.

My father's participation in our lives was intermittent and always unpleasant. When his relationship with Dorosera frayed, he would come around. He'd make me sleep outside with the wild dogs and other predators. I told myself that if the hungry lions hadn't touched me during the long walk from Rwanda to Tanzania, the wild dogs wouldn't harm me, either. Many nights I woke up shivering from the cold. My father often came outside and beat me until he got tired. No wonder some of my siblings had run away. I would still get up in the morning to do my chores, bruised or not. It was always a relief to me when my father patched things up with Dorosera and left again.

Although my aspirations for a quality education seemed impossibly out of reach, I could not stop thinking about school. I had no school uniform, compulsory for admission to school, and no means to buy one. I had no books or other supplies. But a voice inside reminded me that there is a time for everything — a time to cry, and a time to smile. One Sunday morning, I decided it was time to start smiling: I would start school on Monday. To get my father to agree, I told him that the camp commandant had announced that any child found at home and not in school during his camp tour the next day would be thrown into prison. When the commandant said that something was so, no parent disagreed. I promised that I would find a way to balance my duties at home with school. I didn't need to worry that my father would realize I was the only one of his children attending school and question my claim that it was mandatory. My siblings were often away from home for extended periods, escaping our father's violence, and he never knew where they'd gone or cared to find out what they were doing. And as it turned out, the camp commandant soon became tough on kids who were not going to school, even throwing some in jail. Those who were as determined to avoid school as I was to go knew when the commandant was likely to look for them and would escape him by hiding in the bushes or being far from camp, looking for food.

I was both excited and nervous about finally starting school, and I thought it would be better to have someone attend with me. I approached my friend Gahima. Gahima was my neighbour, and we shared many common experiences. Many of the other kids I knew in the camp had two parents who cared about them, and I never believed they would understand what I endured from my father. Gahima lived with her father and stepmother. She wasn't certain, but she thought her birth mother died in the war. Gahima had a good relationship with her father, but her stepmother mistreated her. Sometimes, when her stepmother refused to give her food, Gahima would shrug it off, saying she understood. After all, her father's wife was not her mother. Her relationship with her stepmother gave us a connection. Gahima and I talked about these things and everything else in our lives. It helped to have someone listen. I wanted her with me when I started school, but Gahima said she couldn't even think about it. Her stepmother expected her to do all the household chores and would never allow Gahima to spend any of her time studying. "Telling her about school will spell more trouble for me," she said, "and I have enough of that already!"

I would not be discouraged so easily. Gahima had recently received a letter from a boy who liked her. It took us a long time to find someone who could read the letter to us, and that person had shared the contents of the letter with others in the camp. "Imagine if your dad finds out that you have been receiving love letters from boys," I said. "I wonder what would happen to you." I could see Gahima thinking that if she learned to read, she could keep any future letters to herself. "Let's go to school," I urged. "When we know how to read and write the basic stuff, we can quit."

"How will I approach my stepmother and tell her about school?" Gahima asked. "I know she will say no. Have you talked to *your* parents about it?" I explained to her what I'd told my parents. We planned that Gahima would come and get me once her father came home, and we would tell him and her stepmother about the camp commandant's supposed order. But at seven that evening, she dashed into our tent in excitement. She'd already spoken with her father.

"Papa said yes! He told me that he doesn't need my stepmother's approval, and he has promised to buy books for me in the morning."

"Gahima, I am so happy for you!" I was happy for both of us.

"I know you don't have books, but don't worry," she said. "I will share mine with you."

That night, I washed my lovely blue dress, part of clothes that had been donated by the UNHCR, and hung it to dry on a tree near our tent. I hid it between the branches, so it did not draw the attention of a thief. I woke up many times during the night, wishing the morning sun would hurry up and rise.

When dawn finally broke, I picked up the jerrycan with excitement. I planned to wake Gahima up on my way to get water. Instead, I met her heading to my tent to wake *me* up. We fetched the water and returned home as quickly as we could. Chattering like two little birds, we washed our faces and feet in the morning dew and were ready for school.

Gahima's father bought her notebooks and a pencil from a refugee named Tuyambaze who had connections and owned a small shop. We had two schools to choose from, Kajaho and Rwamurunga. According to village talk, the one in Kajaho was better, but it was three hours away, so we settled for Rwamurunga, which was a one-hour walk away. Walking an hour to school and back again was completely natural to me. I knew that if I kept walking, kept trying to attend school, I would reach my goal of getting some kind of education.

We reached the school with the punctual students and had time before class started. We decided to tour the classrooms to find a comfortable place to sit. Some classrooms had red desks, while others had nothing in them but a chalkboard.

At seven thirty, the timekeeper rang the bell. All the other kids began running in the same direction. Gahima and I didn't know where they were going and wondered if something terrible had happened. One girl called to us to join the group for what was called assembly. Before we started school each day, we had to line up according to our classes, boys in one line and girls in another. We told another student that it was our first time attending school, and they directed us to line up with the other primary one girls. Primary school consisted of primary one to primary seven, the equivalent of grades one to seven in North America. Many students completed only primary school, and some did not even get as far as primary seven. After primary school came high school, which in Uganda was known as the ordinary program (O-levels). Senior one to senior four were the equivalent of grades eight to eleven. A student who completed senior four could go on to a trade school but not to college or university. To do that, you had to complete senior five and senior six (A-levels), the equivalent of grades twelve and thirteen.

A girl stood in front of the assembly and led us as we sang the Ugandan national anthem. I recognized it because I had heard my Ugandan cousins sing it when I was young, but I'd thought it was just a song. I didn't know it was the country's anthem, and I didn't know the words.

As they were singing, both teachers and students stood straight with their hands beside their hips. It was a cold morning, and so I was standing with my hands crossed on my chest, trying to keep myself warm. A teacher slapped my hands and showed me how to show respect for the song. I was confused, but I stood at attention and opened my mouth, pretending to sing. When we finished the anthem, we listened to some announcements and watched as one of the teachers punished some kids for misbehaving. They had to lie down on the ground in front of the entire school while the teacher struck their buttocks with a large stick, over and over. I later learned that the man who doled out the punishment was Teacher Alex, the school's beater extraordinaire, an expert in administering corporal punishment. Everyone feared him.

I was in the same class as Gahima. It had a big window without glass, and students sat on the floor. There was a desk for the teacher and a cabinet to keep books and chalk. As we waited for the teacher, my anxiety built.

"Do you think this is the best place for us?" I asked Gahima.

"Let's wait for a week and see what happens," she replied.

Teacher Sarah entered our class carrying a big stick. She wielded it for noisy students and troublemakers. She'd taught the class how to pronounce the alphabet, and now she randomly chose students to recite what they had learned. I hid behind other students while Gahima sat straight, pretending to have all the answers.

"You. Stand up!" She pointed toward me. I thought she was referring to the girl beside me. "I said you, with the blue dress." Full of dread, I made eye contact. "Stand up and tell the class the twenty-four alphabetic letters."

"A, B, C..." I trailed off after the first three letters in Runyankole. I thought Teacher Sarah would have noticed that it was my first time in her class. Instead, she spat in my face and ordered me to kneel and raise my hands in front of the class.

"Look at your age and size!" she yelled. "You are a big for nothing! How can you fail at reciting the alphabet? You are wasting your time in school. It would be better for you to go home, fetch water for your mother, and get married. Maybe you will be good at taking care of kids and watching after your husband, but school is not for you!"

I felt humiliated, and tears welled in my eyes, but I dared not shed them in front of the class. I could see Gahima watching with trembling lips and stopped looking at her so that she would not become the teacher's next victim. Teacher Sarah called on another younger student to do the recitation, and the student did it perfectly. The kids who knew how to recite the alphabet laughed while those who had no clue watched with trepidation. After four different students had recited the alphabet, Teacher Sarah allowed me to stand up from my punishment.

"During break time, get these kids to teach you the alphabet," she said. "And be ready to recite it in front of the class tomorrow."

I knew I could not spend another day in Teacher Sarah's class. I would have to change to the other class of primary one students or attend the other school. As the rest of the students played outside the classroom during break time, I told Gahima that I was going home.

"I can no longer attend Teacher Sarah's class. I don't think she likes me, and she broke my heart in my first class."

"And what will you tell your mother when she discovers that you ran away from school?"

"I will sit in the bushes and wait until the bell rings for everyone to go home," I said. "When the kids are ready to go home, I will join them."

"Let's go together then," Gahima said.

"I think Teacher Sarah must be from a family that hates girls," I said. I had hoped my first female teacher would encourage me and help me succeed. In the years since, I've wondered if she, too, had survived a trauma. Maybe she felt she had to outdo her male colleagues in severity to students. Either way, she crushed me. Humiliating a young girl just starting her schooling is a deplorable thing to do.

We hid by a swamp, waiting for school to end. I spotted a mango tree across the swamp, and since we were both hungry and without food, we decided to see if any were ripe. On our way to the mango tree, we met a woman carrying cassava. We told her that we were famished. The woman felt sorry for us and gave us two cassava tubers that we ate raw while we sat at the roadside. She didn't question why we weren't in school. Neither of us had official school uniforms, and Gahima had hidden her books in her dress, so the woman probably didn't think we were students.

When the final bell rang, we joined the happy students heading back to our village in the camp. When I reached home, my mother was away, and I guessed she was searching for food. I trekked for an hour into the hills to find firewood. That chore was not always easy. If someone caught you collecting firewood in their area without permission, they would flog you and send you home empty-handed. I had been abused most of my life, but it amazed me that a chore as simple as collecting firewood could put me in harm's way. It made me feel I did not belong in the world.

The following day, Gahima and I returned to school. After the daily assembly, we joined the other class. Teacher Jovia was in charge of this class. While waiting for her arrival, I made friends with some of the other students, hoping they would teach me the alphabet. I didn't want to be embarrassed in front of the class again. I could tell I was much older than most of my classmates, and in not knowing the alphabet, I feared that I was already failing. I took the opportunity to ask what the teacher was like.

"If she likes you, she is the best teacher, but if she doesn't like you, you are in trouble. Unfortunately, teachers here like kids from rich families better than ones from poor homes, and clever kids better than stupid ones."

I was sitting close to a boy named Twahirwa. He was from my village in the camp and well-known as very smart and exceptional in many subjects, especially math. I told him it was my first day and I didn't know anything. He offered to help me during the break times. In exchange, he suggested that I could teach him to speak Runyankole.

Teacher Jovia entered the class with a big stick in her hands, and I panicked. The fear of failing to answer her questions correctly flooded my heart. The entire class stood up and greeted her in English, the language the class was learning for that session. I had some exposure to English in the camp. The white workers couldn't speak Kinyarwanda, so they used English and relied on Kinyarwanda interpreters.

"Good morning, madam!"

"Good morning! How are you? Sit down, everyone."

Unlike Teacher Sarah, Teacher Jovia realized that I was new in the class and asked me to introduce myself. After the previous day, my expectations were low. The thought that I had what my culture would call an empty head, an inherent stupidity, because I lacked any formal education, nagged at me. While I was praying for my life in the swamps or waiting for lions to use my skinny bones as toothpicks, other kids my age were going to school. I also wasn't confident that I'd be able to attend school for long. I knew many girls dropped out. My hope, as I'd suggested to Gahima, was to attend long enough learn to read and write. Without that knowledge, I knew that people would treat me as ignorant, stupid, and inadequate, and opportunities to make choices about my life would be few and far between.

With all that in mind, I didn't want the other students to know too much about me. Instead of sharing my name, I told them my name was Godance and that I came from Kazinga village in the refugee camp. I had no official documentation of my name. Such documents did not exist. When a student took their national exam, they had to give a specific name to receive a mark, but otherwise names were very fluid. As I've said, people were typically known by many different names, and to this day when I go home, I'm called different names by different people. Only in 1993 did the government begin implementing protocols to ensure that everyone had an official first and last name. No one who knew me from the camp challenged me when I called myself Godance.

Teacher Jovia taught us how to add numbers. She wrote some numbers on the blackboard and asked if anyone could add them correctly. Twahirwa raised his hand and answered. She presented a new math exercise on the board and asked for my solution. Twahirwa whispered the answer to me in Kinyarwanda, and I answered. Everyone clapped. The other students looked at me with admiration, and my confidence soared. I was well aware that I got the answer from Twahirwa, but I realized that if I put in some hard work and could answer correctly on my own, I would be respected and heard.

I knew brilliant people who couldn't read or write. Gramma could use her hands to change a baby's position in the womb and had saved countless lives. Was it better to learn from books and teachers with sticks or from older generations steeped in wisdom and experience? Gramma was a vital and revered part of the community. What could I do in my community if I had an education?

EIGHT

The Magic Shoes

Twahirwa and I lived in the same part of the camp, and I often visited him in the evenings for extra coaching. I was determined to make anyone who thought I wouldn't make it feel ashamed for doubting me. Twahirwa helped me for eight months. He'd read illustrated stories to me and then tell me to read them on my own and come back and tell them to him. At first I couldn't understand the words on the page or connect them to the pictures, but I memorized the sight of words, and by paying attention to the pictures in the book, I began to be able to piece parts of the stories together. Within the year, I could read English at a rudimentary level, probably the equivalent of a grade two student. Because I had no notebooks, I tried to memorize everything taught in class while other students took notes. They could review their notes to prepare for exams. Ever resourceful and eager to learn, I would go to my friends' homes so I could read their notes, too.

Juggling school work and home responsibilities was not easy. On Saturdays and Sundays, I often helped my mother in the garden or worked in other people's gardens to get beans, matooke, and cassava to take home to my family. On weekdays, I attended school as much as possible, but sometimes I had to miss days to find food. On the days I could go to school, I often struggled to arrive on time. Every morning I would wake up and then sweep our compound, fetch water, and do chores in the house before I got ready for school. Getting to school late meant suffering a beating. There was no possibility of explaining to the teachers, and even if I had told them why I was so often late, they wouldn't have cared.

Shortly after my first exams, Teacher Jovia prepared our end-of-year report cards. A report card cost five hundred Ugandan shillings, or about fifty cents, which I could not afford. I explained this to my teacher.

"I don't think you need a report card," she said. "If you want, I can show you where you are in the rankings if you plan to tell your parents. Bear in mind that is not for anyone else but you. But don't worry; all the rankings will be announced in class tomorrow from first to last. We have to announce the losers so the class will know who the stupid students in the class are."

That day, I went home dejected. Gahima promised to divide her notebook next term and share half with me. Maybe that would improve my performance. The night passed quickly, but I didn't want to go to school. I remembered a saying in Swahili, "Kama mbaya mbaya" — "Whatever happens, happens!" I prepared to go to school and face whatever was in store for me.

The school had a ceremony where all the teachers sat in one line and the students were invited in. Sometimes parents were invited to attend as well. The top three students got the privilege of shaking hands with all of the teachers and the parents. After the ceremony, the students would go back to class and the teachers would hand out the report cards.

I arrived late. Many students, anticipating excellent grades, were excited to get their report cards. Teacher Jovia called the names of the top three students and they joined her at the front of the class while the other students cheered for them. Teacher Jovia continued to announce each student's position, from the best down to the worst. My class had fifty students. I sat in the corner as she called one name after another, none of them mine.

"Now it is time to announce the last person in the class," she said. "Number fifty... Godance!" All the students turned in my direction with screams of derision and mocking laughter. I wanted to run, but there was no place to go. "You'd better go and help your mother at home instead of wasting your time coming to school," Teacher Jovia said. "Or you should get married and take care of your husband and children. But your kids will be the same. They will always be at the bottom of the class like you."

How did I hold back my tears? I blocked my ears. I was utterly humiliated. I remembered how Peteronira, a woman living next to our tent, tried to convince my father to stop me from attending school. "School is not for girls," she said. "When they go to school, they don't study but spend their time with boys and get a grandbaby as a certificate."

My life was full of pain and I needed to unload that burden. Silently, I spoke to God. God, if you exist, why didn't you allow me to die in the forest? Why did the hungry lions spare me? If you knew that I was going to suffer in this world, why did you create me? I think you answer other people's prayers and ignore mine. God, this is your fault, and that's why when I call, you close your ears and don't want to listen to my voice.

Twahirwa made a path through my jeering classmates so I could leave. When I got home, the news that I was the last in my class had spread. My father came to our tent and told me he'd heard of my poor performance. "You are not going to school anymore," he said. "But if you insist, you will have to find another place to live. There is work for you to do at home, and you will stop wasting your time in school."

During the holiday, I tried my best to make enough money to purchase books. Every day, I got up at three o'clock and walked to Kyabishaho, where I searched for work tending people's gardens. The trek took four hours in the morning and four hours back each evening. I visited most houses in the village, asking if they had any jobs for me. If I was lucky, someone would give me a menial job to do. They often paid me not with the money I so badly needed but with beans, cassava, matooke, and other food items. Sometimes, people would pay me with two large matooke weighing around fifteen kilos each. They were very heavy, but I had no choice but to place them on my head for the four-hour walk home. Between the hours of walking, the menial labour, and neither breakfast nor lunch to sustain me, I would fall asleep under a tree on my way home. When I woke up, I would have to wait for someone to help place the matooke back on my head. I repeated the same pattern day in and day out and soon lost most of my hair from carrying such heavy loads on my head. When the opportunity arose, I would sell some of the food items. I used some of the money to buy things we needed at home, especially salt and soap. I also saved enough to purchase four books required for the new term: math, English, social studies, and science. By the time the new term was about to start, I was determined to pull myself together and concentrate on my studies as much as I could. Starting fresh was hard, but my return stunned the kids who had laughed at me at the end of the last term. Unfortunately, at home I still had chores to do, and again I was habitually late. Many mornings after chores my father administered a severe beating before I left for school. Sometimes, I was so sore that I would have to stand in class for the whole day.

I attended school for three days each week. The remaining two days I spent trying to get food for my family. Often I arrived home to find only an empty cooking pot waiting for me. In my culture, if someone visits you while you are eating, it is customary to invite them to dine with you. Sometimes, if you knew your neighbour was cooking, you would visit their house and pretend to listen to their conversation, all the while waiting for them to share their food. Kids often went house to house trying to fill their bellies. Parents didn't discourage those visits. Many struggled to provide for their children, especially larger families. It was impossible for a refugee family to feed twelve children every day. Kids learned to take care of themselves.

It was hard to find food some days, and I would travel for several hours but return empty-handed. Other days were better. We had a superstition that if a rat began crossing the road in front of you and turned back when it saw you, it was a bad omen, and you would be wise to return home. That happened to me often, but instead of returning home, I would go to the forest and collect firewood and then head to another camp village and visit ten to twenty houses, looking for someone who would take the firewood in exchange for food. Most of the time, people would say no or would offer me a small amount of food that was not worth the firewood they took. Imagine trading thirty kilos of firewood for two kilos of beans! But the thought of returning home with the firewood on my head meant that I usually settled for the unfair exchange. At least we could cook the beans for dinner and worry about tomorrow later. I had to study hard to make up for the days I was away from school.

One morning, I woke up to the sound of rain pouring down in torrents. Nonetheless, I packed my books, secured them in my clothes, and headed to school. By the time I was halfway, the rain had soaked my clothes, and my books were sodden. My books meant everything to me. How would I buy new ones? I cried until I reached school. And to make matters worse, when I checked my books after I arrived, all my notes were gone.

When the teacher came in, she wrote notes on the chalkboard for us to copy. Everyone started writing. I hid in the back of the class in my drenched clothes, pretending to write. When the teacher asked for my work, I told her the rain destroyed my books. Immediately, she ordered me out of her class. I intended to learn no matter what, so for the rest of that lesson I stood behind a window where no one could see me (I didn't want another teacher to catch me) and peeped through a small hole in the window. The next day, I missed school because I had to find money to purchase new books. After about a week and half, I went to the Red Cross to explain why I couldn't attend school. They gave me some books, pencils, pens, and a uniform. I loved my pink uniform. I wanted to look smart, so I ironed it with a metal cup. I would put hot coals in the cup, tie it with a cloth, and iron it on a blanket. It worked so well that no one could tell I had ironed it with a cup! My mother shaved my hair with a razor blade or a pair of scissors. She was skilled, and I suffered no nicks or scrapes. I really looked like a student, although I was still barefoot. Before the war, I had a pair of shoes that I wore to church, the market, and when visiting family friends, but I was barefoot when Elijah and I fled, and I never got another pair. If someone had given me shoes, I don't think I'd have known how to put them on.

I studied every moment I could, carrying a book everywhere, even when I used the toilet (the camp finally had toilets) or searched for firewood. I stopped playing games with other kids so I could focus on reading.

I had been learning English at school, but listening to music made me fall in love with the language. My favourite song in school helped me pronounce some English words for the first time. I learned them quickly because they were translated into Runyankole: "House, *Enyumba*; banana, *matooke*; cup, *ekyikopo*; elephant, *ejonjo*; fish, *ekyenyanja*; and girl, *omuhaara!*" I loved learning.

As I worked hard and learned in school, the teachers gradually started to treat me better. On this day, Teacher Jovia proudly announced that I was number ten in my class and had earned promotion to primary two. When the new semester began, I studied even harder, and by the end of the term I ranked second, right below Twahirwa! Nobody, not even me, could believe I had secured second place. I was so proud that I could compete with boys. I thought that if I didn't have to miss school each week to feed my family, I could even beat Twahirwa. At the end of each term, the school awarded prizes to the top three students in each class. The first-place student received a basin, a plate, and a cup. The second-place prize was a set of plates and some cups, and the third-place student received a cup and some books. Teacher Sarah presented the prizes, and I shook her hand firmly as a confirmation that I had remained strong despite what she'd done to me on my very first day. It soon became common knowledge that the prizes for my class would go to three people: Twahirwa, Mukansoro, and me.

Gahima decided she could no longer handle the teachers' abuse and dropped out of school. In a wonderful turn of events, Gahima found out a year later that her mother had not died in the war. She eventually reunited with her, and they lived together for a time. A couple of years after that, I heard that Gahima got married. But, in her absence, I made new friends. One day, a tall, gorgeous, and smart girl, Mukansoro, joined our class. When she learned that I was the smartest girl in class, she approached me, and we became friends. She loved playing volleyball and played with students from primary five, six, and seven. She wanted me to join the team, but I declined. I needed to study during my break time.

In the end, I was top of the class so often that my family stopped buying plates, cups, and basins. Eventually, some jealous people in the camp told my father that I would never amount to anything. He tried everything possible to make me quit school, but I ignored him. I endured frequent beatings, and he resorted to picking a fight every night and then shutting Mama and me out of our house. He threatened to burn down the house of anyone who helped us. My mother would sleep at her sister's the whole night. I would sleep outside our tent and leave for school in the morning. I lost count of how many times I slept outside, and still I excelled in school. I gained even more confidence when, in primary four, I joined the debate club. I had doubted Him before, and I still questioned His presence in my most desperate moments, but I knew God was on my side, and His spirit kept moving me forward.

I could not afford to eat breakfast or lunch in the school canteen. I once followed some of my friends to the canteen in hopes they would share their food with me. I knew they had parents who could afford to give them money. Bananas cost two hundred shillings, or about twenty-five cents. The girls bought bananas. I swallowed every time they chewed. As they ate, I counted the remaining bananas, hoping they would offer one to me. Finally, every banana was gone. I wanted to be like them, but that was impossible. My father didn't care, and my mother didn't have the means.

It was a Sunday morning, and I was still sleeping when my sister Godance dashed into the tent. "Wake up! Wake up!" she shouted.

"Please leave me alone," I replied. "I am not going to church today."

"No, wake up and see this! I think we are rich!" I opened my eyes and saw a new money note in her hands. Godance had found it on the ground on her way to the toilet. Drunks staggering home at night routinely dropped money, and people often woke up early to comb the common routes. She had hesitated at first and then picked up the note and ran home.

"How much is it?" she asked excitedly.

I counted with my fingers. "Twenty thousand shillings!" I said. At the time, that was worth almost eight Canadian dollars — a fortune. I could have told her it was worth two thousand shillings and pocketed the difference, but she came to me because she trusted me, and I valued that. Godance struggled to comprehend the value of what she'd found. We sat and dreamed about the beautiful things we could purchase with the money, like shoes and dresses. We loved clothes with beautiful flowers, similar to the ones we saw on rich kids. Although Godance was taller than me, we agreed to buy things of the same colour to look like twins.

We told Mama of Godance's discovery. Godance was scared Mama would take the money from us, but she only advised us to spend it wisely.

"Buy something you have been dreaming of," Mama said. "God gave you that money. Please keep it a secret. If your father knows about it, he will take the money away from you."

The market opened once a week on Thursdays. That week, I prayed for market day to come quickly. Godance and I woke up early. It was not a day for school; it was a day to shop! As we stood waiting for the market to open, Mama arrived. She came to inspect what we bought and ensure everything fit perfectly. There was no return policy, so if you purchased clothes and later realized they were too small or too big, you were out of luck.

When the stalls finally opened, we located a person selling some colourful dresses. We picked out dresses with red flowers and tried them on. They were perfect. Mama bargained with the sellers, and we paid twelve thousand shillings. Then the search for shoes started. We could only afford shoes that cost four thousand shillings each. We searched tirelessly for ones that would match our dresses. Toward the end of the day, we found a seller with the shoes we loved. They were black flats with laces and closed toes.

As we headed home, I could hardly contain my joy, and the walk back felt like it took an eternity. I wanted to show my friends that God had remembered me. I did not know who had dropped the note or what its loss might have meant to them, but I told myself that one man's problem is another's blessing. I thanked God for answering our prayers and giving us the money.

At home, I put my new dress and shoes on right away and started practising so I could walk to the Sunday service without falling. I was not used to shoes. "Are they too big? Too small?" I asked Mama.

"I think you will make this dress old before you wear it," she said as I paced around the tent.

The following Sunday, we timed it so that we arrived at church late. I wanted everyone else sitting down as we entered. When we walked in, all eyes turned to us. People started asking us if it were Christmastime. But then I noticed that some people were laughing. At first, I thought they were jealous, but then I started feeling uncomfortable.

"Do you know why people are laughing at you?" a woman asked us. "You wore your shoes on the wrong feet!"

"What!" I exclaimed.

"I can show you how to wear them properly if you like."

I was mortified but thankful to the kind woman. It took me a long time to learn which shoe goes on the left foot and which goes on the right. Sometimes, when I got it wrong and people laughed at me, I would pull my shoes off and hold them in my hands. If anyone asked me why I was walking barefoot, I would tell them that my shoes were too small.

A few days later, Murora, a hard-working friend with the lofty dream of becoming a businesswoman, came to me in tears. She sold tomatoes at the Kajaho market and saved money with the hope of one day owning a proper shop. Her bank was a plastic bag she kept in a hole in the wall of her house. One day, she opened the hiding place to count her money only to discover that rats had torn all the notes to pieces. When she told me she'd lost two years' worth of savings, we sobbed together. I searched for comforting words.

"I understand your pain, but that money was never yours," I said. "If something is yours, nobody can take it from you. Maybe something bad was going to happen to you after you opened your shop. Maybe thieves were going to take all your money and leave you dead."

Murora struggled to understand, but a few days later she told me the talk had changed her life and she had stopped thinking about the money. She believed that God would provide her with ways to get more money. I was glad Murora could see life that way.

When I was in primary four, a new obstacle to my school attendance unexpectedly emerged. I had just stood up at the beginning of lunchtime to get water to drink from the borehole when my friend immediately ordered me to sit.

"Your cloth is soiled with blood," she said. "Maybe you are on your period." I had no idea what she meant. "I will tell you after everyone is gone," she promised. When all the students had left the classroom, she explained menstruation. "This blood is a sign that you are mature and can start having kids."

"What?" My eyes widened with shock.

"You have to be very careful now. If you have sex with any man, you will get pregnant."

"How can I get pregnant when I am unmarried?"

"Some girls sleep with boys and then get pregnant," she replied. "I think you must have seen such girls around."

I never chased boys, so I didn't worry about getting pregnant that way. But I knew that sometimes a girl could become pregnant when a boy or man raped her. I prayed to God that such evil would not befall me, knowing that I would be the one blamed.

That day, I sat for hours so nobody would see my red-stained uniform. After class, I told my friends that I would be staying back to do some extra reading. When it was dark, I rose and went home. I arrived home at around eight and told my parents that I had stopped to collect firewood in someone's garden after school but that the owner had seized it. I kept my period a secret because I did not want them to think for a second that I was old enough to get married.

I had never seen sanitary pads before, and even if I knew what they were, I had no money to buy them. All through my days in primary school, I had no underwear. Underwear was a costly luxury. I could only afford a pair of short pants to wear under my dress. Now, when it was time for my period, I would feign sickness and miss school for three days. I was lucky that no one in my family bothered to ask probing questions.

By the time I was fourteen, most of the girls in my class had quit school. Some left to get married. Others, like Gahima, abandoned their studies because the teachers were so abusive. Girls had obligations at home that boys didn't have, and as I well knew, trying to balance studying and chores was exhausting. One by one, girls started to drop out of school, and in the end, few refugee girls remained. I didn't blame them. It was hard to be a female student. Some of the male teachers coerced girls into sex, and if the girls got pregnant, they had to leave school. Nothing happened to the teachers, of course. The hygiene days were another ordeal and one ripe for abuse. The female teachers would take the older girls one by one to a room and check to make sure we were clean. They checked every part of our bodies. One male teacher in particular was always around when we were being checked. Only the female students were subjected to this humiliation. Nobody inspected the boys. And when the school provided each girl with three cloth pads that could be washed and reused, the teachers would openly tell you to check to make sure your pad was clean. When I knew a hygiene day was looming, I made sure to arrive late. I'd rather have been smacked for tardiness than suffer the indignity of inspection. I became the only girl in the class. No one cared about the girls who quit. School was meant for boys.

NINE

The Lost Girl

All around me, girls my age were getting married. My older sister, Uwimpuhwe, had married at sixteen solely to escape our father's violence. This episode started when my father hit my mother and then went after my siblings and me. We all fled. Uwimpuhwe and I hid, and she told me that she was leaving and she wasn't coming back. I pressed her to tell me where she was going, and eventually she told me that she planned to stay with a friend in another village in the camp. That night I went home to see if my mother was still alive. It was a sad reality that I became accustomed to the routine of the fights, the flights, and the fears for my mother's life. I found her nursing her bruises and heated some water in the hopes that a bath would ease her pain.

A week later, someone came to tell us that Uwimpuhwe was married. My father went to demand a dowry from her new husband's family, but they had nothing to give. My father demanded the return of his daughter, but Uwimpuhwe refused to leave. My father disowned her and told us to never see her again. He said he would kumuca her, which meant she had dishonoured us and would not be welcomed in the family again.

As much as I wanted to escape my father's violence, too, Uwimpuhwe's solution did not appeal to me. I often vehemently rejected offers of marriage. Jack, a married man at least twice my age with two children, would flirt with me on my way home from school. He said that he had talked with my father and was willing to pay whatever he wanted for my dowry. He pestered me for weeks. Privately, I vowed that if my father forced me to marry him, I would flee and start a new life in another village. I prayed to God to let me finish primary seven. I had no plans to continue to secondary school. You had to pay tuition to attend secondary school, and I couldn't afford it.

As the last refugee girl in my class, I was lonely and tempted to quit, but I knew this was my chosen fight. At the same time, I felt trapped, suspended in an ocean of uncertainties. As much as I loved to learn, attending school was a struggle. My father beat me for attending, the school beat me each time I was absent, and my empty stomach made studying hard. I was always exhausted, and if I nodded off in class, the teacher would abruptly strike me on the head with a cane to wake me. I developed a permanent headache from those cane strikes. My grandmother would heat an iron bar in the fire until it glowed red and then lay it on my forehead to make the headache go away. I have numerous scars from those treatments.

Although I loved learning, I hated school, I hated being at home, and I hated my community. Now, the pressure was building to live a life that was not of my choosing. People told me that my father beating me was a sign that I was getting old and should start my own family. I heard this so often that I started believing them. At times I almost gave in. But deep down, I knew that marriage wasn't what I wanted, and I held firm. I had a feeling that something else was meant for me.

I did not want a marriage like my parents' and other women in the village. When I thought of marriage, all I could see was an abusive husband and a new occupation as caretaker. I didn't like how wives did everything in the home while their husbands came home drunk and beat them. Many things broke my heart, but seeing a woman beaten in front of her children was the worst. I always wondered if the sons would grow up to beat their wives. Who would break the circle of violence against women?

I prayed harder for a solution, but again God did not seem to be listening. I was desperate for a source of happiness. As a child, music was always in my heart. Music and singing seemed magical to me. I'd seen babies smile when music filled the air around them. If a melody could make babies smile, then how much better would it be for someone like me, with a sense of understanding? The church had three different choir groups, and I joined the one called the Reapers. The choir was a group of men, women, girls, and boys, and we held our singing practices twice a week, on Wednesday and Saturday evenings. Singing in the choir made such a difference in my life that people began to comment on the change in me. Just that little bit of happiness twice a week put a smile on my face. I must have impressed the other members, too, because they asked me to serve as the choir treasurer. For several months, I kept the choir's money and delivered frequent financial reports.

Inspired by my enterprising friend Murora, I decided to build a tomato business of my own. I decided to use the choir's money to fund the purchase of two boxes of tomatoes that I could then sell at the Thursday market. I anticipated huge profits that would allow me to return the choir's money immediately.

Unfortunately, before market day came, someone from the choir found out and reported me to the president. The president asked me to bring the money to choir practice the next day. I dashed to Murora's house and begged her to lend me some cash, promising to return her money very soon.

The next day at choir practice, I confidently produced the money and the books to show that everything was intact. At the market, I sold all of the tomatoes, making a profit of five dollars. With the proceeds, I bought two new boxes and sold those. I paid off all my debts (school friends would sometimes loan me money so I could buy something for lunch), including the loan from Murora, and bought one more tomato box. Instead of missing two days of school each week to search for food for my family, now I missed only Thursdays, when I sold tomatoes at the market. I loved the business of selling and thought I would like to be a businesswoman. I knew, however, that I was unlikely to be able to defy my community's expectations forever. Marriage was in my future, and then my only job would be to take care of my husband and children. But for now, for the first time in my life, I had money in my pocket. Selling tomatoes was not just about creating a stream of income; it meant I could afford the basic things I needed.

I took some of the money I made at the market and bought Kotex pads. They were expensive, but I was tired of staying in bed for three days every month. I also purchased some underwear, toothpaste, and my first body lotion, called Movit. I was using cooking oil to moisturize my skin and wanted a cream that, I hoped, would take away my scars.

After the episode with the tomatoes and the choir money, I told the choir executive that I no longer wanted to serve as treasurer. When it was time to elect the new executive, however, someone nominated me to be president. When I learned that I was one of three nominees, I laughed it off as a joke. The president's role was tiring, and dealing with people older than me would make it even harder. I was certain that no one would vote for me. I was busy reading the Bible when our president, Byaruhanga, called everyone to attention. They had counted all the ballots. "The new president of the choir for 2001 is Kadur," he said.

I was so shocked that I immediately asked why they chose me over the other candidates. "You are young, and we believe you will do very well in this position," one of the other members explained. "You are very punctual at meetings, and you are the one lady in the choir who speaks some English. The fact that you also speak other languages means you could help visitors who can't speak Kinyarwanda. Above all, you present yourself well."

My active participation in English class and the debate club had paid off. I felt comfortable speaking in front of people, especially when singing in church. But now, I had a lot on my plate. I was busy preparing for my national primary school examination, leading the church choir, and selling tomatoes on Thursdays.

In 2001, when I was fifteen, I was ready to sit the national examination. The school told us that on the day of the exam we would have to stay inside the exam room. No one could go home to eat or to the canteen to buy lunch; if we brought money to pay for it, the school would provide food. But I faced an additional and unexpected challenge: my father had kicked me out of the tent. I had to leave behind all my notes and books, and my father refused to give them to me. The leader of our village tried to intervene.

"Even if the ground turns to blood, there is no way I can give her those books," my father said. "Her older sister is married, and she is wasting time in school, which does not make any sense to me. I will see how she will do in her exam without her books. She will come last." And he laughed. He laughed at me. I wanted to cry, but I did not want to cry in front of him because I knew my tears made him happy.

I hoped to find someone who would take me in, even just for a week, while I studied for the exam. My grandparents couldn't do it. Their house was so tiny it barely fit the two of them. My mother advised me to reach out to my aunt Grace, who had come to the camp a couple of years earlier when she learned we were living there. She lived in another village about an hour's walk from our tent. "My daughter," Mama said, "you are a hard-working girl, and I believe your aunt will take you in. I know if you wake up early and do all the chores, she will allow you to stay with her for a few days until you finish your exam. You can also ask her to get a loan for you, and when you are done with your exam, you can work to pay it back."

That evening, I walked to my aunt's. Many times I knelt down and prayed, raising my arms high. That day, God listened to me. My aunt and uncle allowed me to stay. I borrowed books from my Ugandan classmates. If one was studying science, she would lend me her social studies book for a few hours.

When exam day came, I felt like my head was empty. As I ironed my uniform with my hot metal cup, shaved my head with scissors, scrubbed my cracked feet, and, because I had run out of lotion, applied cooking oil to my skin, I could not remember what I'd learned. I walked to school with nothing in my hands except a blue pen my aunt gave me. Other students' parents came with them and wished them luck. I was alone, but my mother wished me the best, and my aunt prayed for me. That morning, before I left, she told me she had dreamed that I'd triumphed in the exams. "Not everything we dream can come true," I told her.

The students of Kajaho and Rwamurunga Primary Schools wrote the exams together. None of the female students looked like me. I could tell that some had their hair cut with proper clippers. I watched them going through their notes and quizzing each other but felt too self-conscious to ask anyone to lend me their notes.

At eight o'clock, the students lined up. The teachers in charge were strangers to me. They did not look friendly at all. They rarely did. They checked one by one to see if we had hidden notes anywhere. We had to raise our arms so they could check in our armpits. They also told us to open our mouths so they could peer inside. They even checked our underwear.

We went inside the classroom, where wooden school benches were arranged in three rows. The benches could hold two students, but we sat alone. One teacher stood at the back and another at the front carefully watched us. They'd disqualify you if you tried to make eye contact with a classmate. The head teacher came into the room with the first exam: science. When it was time to start, I opened the exam booklet and found fifty-two questions. The first told me to "Give one reason why a child's diet should have more protein than that of an adult." Do children need protein? I wondered. Maybe the rich kids do. Poor kids eat whatever they can get. I answered the question as best I could, though none of the questions seemed relevant to me. I thought they would be fine for kids whose parents helped them or who had lots of time to prepare. After that came the English exam.

The next day we started with math, and in the evening we wrote the social studies exam. The sixteenth question instructed me to give one reason why the British decided to settle in Kenya. I didn't remember studying this in class, but maybe it was taught when I was absent. I did not even touch my pen to the paper. I wondered why they were asking questions about the British. I expected them to ask about Uganda. When the exam was over, we started talking about the questions. I asked another student about the sixteenth question, and she confirmed that they'd studied it when I was away.

"So do you know the answer?" I asked.

"When the white settlers came to Kenya, they settled in the Highlands because there was good fertile land for their farms. Non-Europeans were displaced and did not have anywhere to go."

I was annoyed. I thought, why do we need to study English? Do the English care about learning our languages? Of course not because what good would our languages do them? They are so sure we are less than them, just because of our skin tone.

The exam lasted for two days. When it came time to complete the forms identifying which secondary schools I hoped to attend, I told Mr. Mbonyi that I didn't think I could attend high school. He was a blessed figure in my eyes. Although he beat us sometimes, he was never untoward to the girls, and we all saw him as a parent figure who looked out for his students. I was surprised many years later to learn that he never had children of his own.

"Why not?" he asked.

"My parents won't be able to pay for my fees. I am the only person in my family that has finished primary school."

"Every student must complete that form," he said. "It is a requirement. Just fill in the blank with any secondary school that comes to mind."

I went home and filled in the form. There were three secondary schools in my area: Rwamuranga, Kajaho, and Kyabirukwa. I put them all down and added schools from the Isingiro district for good measure.

I was proud of what I had achieved. Being the only refugee girl in my class made me believe I was a fighter. I waited for my exam results with no expectations; I knew I couldn't go higher. I concentrated on my responsibilities in the church choir and my tomato business. I learned that people assumed that now that I was finished with school, I'd get married. Jack wasn't the only man who approached my father and tried to convince him to let me marry them. Some plied him with alcohol. Some were almost my father's age! I started coming home early to avoid men kidnapping me. I stopped trusting my friends. I chose to be lonely. I wanted to be free. I wanted to play hide and seek. I wanted to explore. I wanted to enjoy life on my own terms, but I was born a girl.

I hoped that spending time at the church would protect me. The choir went on a three-day trip to Kyezimbire. Choirs from many different regions participated. We spent an amazing first day worshipping and singing, and I found it very healing. One pastor described God as the father of the fatherless, the father of all orphans. I was not an orphan, and yet I felt more than an orphan. A line in one particular song touched my heart: "Are you weary, are you heavy-hearted? Tell it to Jesus!"

That evening, when church was done, we went to dinner. After dinner, we went to the houses near the church where we would sleep: women in one house, and men in another. When we were ready for bed, one pastor called a girl named Mukamana to him. "Let me go and see what the pastor wants. Maybe he wants to give me tomorrow's agenda," she said. She left the room, and I fell into bed. I felt like I had been sleeping for just a few minutes when I heard her telling me to wake up. Her lips quivered. I asked her what had happened, but at first she could not speak. Then she said, "The pastor almost raped me!" I could not believe it.

She told me that he'd touched every part of her body. At first she froze in fear, and then she yelled at him and he pushed her to the ground. Somehow she got away from him. She asked me not to say anything. She didn't want the pastor to know she'd shared anything with me. I agreed because I knew that nobody would do a thing to stop him.

I could not wait to go home. For the next two days I looked so unhappy that people asked me what was wrong. I lied and said I was sick. I had respected the church pastors. They used to tell us that they were the ambassadors of Christ on Earth, and I believed them. I decided that when I got home, I would stop going to church.

At last the examination results were available. When I heard that I had passed, I didn't think it could be true. How had I passed when I didn't have my books or my notes or anyone who could help me with my homework? But then I was told to go to the UNHCR office. I had heard rumours about an organization that was going to fund secondary education for the best students, with girls being the priority, but I didn't believe the stories. When I arrived at the office, I met Betty, a girl I knew from Kajaho Primary School. She told me she was the first girl in her class to receive excellent grades. She, too, had heard the rumours about high-school scholarships.

A man from the office called my name and beckoned me to follow him. I felt a tinge of excitement like something extraordinary was about to happen but uncertain as to what exactly it would be. We entered an office where a woman waited for us, and the man asked me to take a seat. When I sat, the woman began asking me questions.

"What do you want to become in life if allowed to study?" she asked.

"That's a hard question, as I cannot predict what the future will look like for me."

"So you don't know what you want in life?"

"I know what I want, but most of my life has been full of surprises."

"Let's say you were sure about your future, and you could design it yourself," she said. "What would your life look like?"

"I wish I could help women in abusive marriages, and end domestic violence against women and girls, and stop teachers from abusing students, and save kids from parental abuse, and advocate for the education of girls all over the world."

"Do you mean human rights?"

"Yes!" I knew this term from the aid workers in the camps. The Right to Play workers told us that it was our right as children to have fun, although that was easier said than done.

"You can study that in university, but you need to work hard to get there. Most kids dream of becoming nurses, doctors, and engineers. Why do you want to become a human rights activist?"

"I am living a life I never chose," I explained. "I have seen innocent people, especially kids, dying in the street. I've seen people living like animals, and I have been so removed from my roots that I've almost forgotten my family's origins. I grew up in this country, but sadly, I returned as a refugee. I want to address some of the ills I see everyday."

The conversation lasted for almost two hours. In the end, the woman handed me a paper to sign and told me that Windle Trust chose me to study at Isingiro Secondary School on a scholarship! I broke down, trembling and sobbing uncontrollably.

"How is this possible?" I asked. "I never thought a person like me would ever get an opportunity to attend secondary school." I was excited and so grateful. But I wondered why they chose Isingiro Secondary School instead of Rwamurunga Secondary School, which was closer to the camp. I knew enough of Isingiro to know this was not a school I could walk to and from each day. The woman explained that I needed to attend a boarding school so that I could concentrate on my studies.

I knew my life was going to change forever. My endless search for food and other supplies was over. No more beatings at home, no more sleeping outside. We shook hands, and she told me when to report to the school.

TEN

Engata

I raced home at top speed, my thumping heart about to burst out of my chest. My momentous news had preceded me. Everyone in my village already knew that I'd received a scholarship to study at Isingiro Secondary School. I would be the first girl from our village or the Kazinga Zone in the refugee camp to attend secondary school, and a boarding school at that. My quiet mother beamed with happiness.

"They are ashamed, those who wanted you to get married. Keep shining. I believe in you, and you will fight for yourself," she told me.

Betty had come out of her interview jumping with excitement. She, too, would be attending Isingiro. We'd each received a list of the supplies we would need to take with us, and we'd arranged to meet at the market that Thursday to shop together. The list included a roll-up mattress, bed sheets, and blankets. I had never slept on a mattress in my life. From my tomato business, I had saved enough to purchase the sheets and blankets. Someone kindly gave me a goat, and I spent hours waiting at the goat sellers' stall in the market before someone bought it for forty thousand shillings.

When I met up with Betty, she had already purchased everything on the list. I thought she must be from a wealthy family, at least compared to mine! I purchased the mattress and bedding I needed. I also bought books and pens. Vestina gave me a metal case to keep my belongings in. It was old and ugly, and I would have liked something new, but at least I had all the basics. God will provide the rest, I told myself. That weekend, I washed my clothes and said goodbye to my friends. I'd be away for three months.

I woke up early on the day of my departure. I'd heard countless stories about students from urban areas teasing and bullying those from rural communities, and I was scared to death of what would happen to me, a Rwandan girl from a refugee camp. Mama asked one of our neighbours with a bicycle to carry my belongings to Kajaho. From Kajaho, Betty and I would take a taxi to the school. When it was time to leave, my mother offered me some advice.

"My daughter, I wish I could stop you from attending school, but I know that's not possible. Who is going to help me around here? You are like my husband, and now you are leaving. I believe you know what our neighbours are saying. They say you are wasting your time, and some believe that you are going away to work in a hotel as a prostitute. Please study hard and prove them wrong. I want to see you wearing a graduation hat. That would put all the haters to shame."

"Mama, don't worry. Most people didn't believe I could finish primary school. But when all the other girls in my class dropped out, God rewarded my hard work with a scholarship. I am lucky to have this opportunity, and I will never treat it as a joke." And I reminded her of a Kinyarwandan expression, "Utazi I yo ava ntamenya I yo agana" — "if you don't know where you come from, you will not know where you are going."

As we spoke, I sobbed. Isingiro was too far from Oruchinga for me to visit her during the term.

Betty was waiting for me at the trading centre. As we got in the taxi, I was nervous, but there was no turning back. Another female student on her way to Isingiro travelled with us along with a man, presumably her father. When we stopped at another trading centre on the way, he bought her a chapati and soda. I was jealous. Watching this girl and her father, I couldn't help thinking about my own. I'd had to try to keep my father from finding out about my scholarship for fear he would stop me from going to boarding school. Fortunately, he'd been sleeping at Dorosera's. He would not have cared if I'd reached my new school safely. Many times I had wondered if he really was my father, but I was too shy to ask my mother. Sometimes I remembered how Buseka had made sure that Elijah and I made it from Rwanda to the refugee camp in Tanzania. If I found another man like him who would take care of me, I thought, I would call him my father, even though my culture believes that no one else can take the place of your father, no matter how useless or dangerous he may be.

At last the taxi reached the school. I looked out the window and saw students playing on the playground. The boys wore white T-shirts and brown pants, and the girls white T-shirts and brown skirts. I pictured myself in the uniform. The taxi stopped at the gate, and we paid the driver.

I stood in front of my new secondary school, and I felt that I, a girl raised in a culture that did not support female achievement, from a poor family with an abusive father, a refugee who had to fight to go to primary school, had achieved the impossible. I had suffered many trials and many tests, and yet there I stood, sixteen years old and ready to begin secondary school. But reaching the peak of the mountain is never the end of the journey.

The gatekeeper pointed us in the direction of the head teacher's office, where we would register. In the schoolyard, some students read under the shade of a big tree. I struggled to carry my heavy metal case full of supplies. The registration officer, Molly, took our names and assigned us our classes. Students in their first year were divided into two classes, North and South. Betty and I were excited to be in the same class, North. Molly had a calm demeanour and a soft voice. She led us to the dormitory. As we walked, I looked around me. The buildings were rundown. The brick walls looked old, the floors were cracked, and the toilets were long troughs we had to squat over. But we had a tiny library and a laboratory, which my primary school never had. The school's motto was *Knowledge is Gold*, which I loved.

Molly told us we could choose any empty bed we wanted. We wanted one close to a window, but those were already claimed. I vowed to get to school early next term so I could choose the best bed. As we made up our beds, Betty complained that the dormitory smelled like rotten eggs. I couldn't smell a thing. At some point in grade four, I'd realized that I'd lost my sense of smell. I could remember smelling the decay of the swamp when Elijah and I hid in the reeds, and the smells of the refugee camp, and then one day the sense was gone. I have no idea why; perhaps one of my father's or my teachers' beatings had injured my brain. I've since had an MRI that revealed nothing.

It was time for lunch and the room began to fill with girls. "We have engata here!" one announced. *Engata* is a word used for new students. She held out her arms to Betty. "Come and hug me," she said. But when Betty drew closer, the girl pushed her away. "Don't touch me!" she screamed. The other students cheered as she called us all sorts of names. "She is a dirty girl from the village. Don't go near her. She will mess your clothes." Betty burst into tears.

"Let's go to lunch!" another girl roared. "In the evening, we shall teach them how to behave in boarding school. They need training so that they can train other newcomers next year."

We were famished, but Betty and I stayed in the dormitory, terrified of what might happen if we stepped out for food. Betty wanted to go home right away, but I said we should wait to see what happened that night and decide then. As on my first day of primary school, I didn't want to just give up, no matter how unwelcome I felt. I had come too far not to give my education my best shot. I spent the rest of the day lying on my bed. A tall, plump girl approached me and ordered me to fetch water for her. "I don't know where to fetch water," I said.

"Go outside and you will see other girls with jerrycans. Follow them. Make sure you hurry, because I need to take a shower as soon as possible." The dormitories were not equipped with running water. We had to collect water ourselves and then shower by pouring the contents of a jerrycan over ourselves or transferring the water to a basin and then scooping up the water with our hands.

I got up and went out to the tap. I saw other girls who were fetching water for more senior students. When I returned to the dormitory, the girl who sent me for water took the jerrycan into the bathroom. I didn't see Betty and assumed she was also running an errand for a senior.

Every evening after dinner, students would go back to their classrooms for prep. Some found it frustrating to spending their evenings studying. We had to wake up at five in the morning each day — and often we woke up as early as four so we could study before breakfast — and evening prep meant we had no time to relax. Even though it was our first day, Betty and I went to prep. We learned from some of the boys that the boys' dormitory was much the same as the girls'. I spent that first evening of prep dreading the idea of returning to the dormitory. Much as I wanted to sleep on a fluffy mattress for the first time in my life, I was scared of the seniors.

I ran to the dormitory and hid under my covers, pretending to be fast asleep, hoping to escape whatever trouble the girls planned. At about one o'clock in the morning, a senior named Bless called all the engatas to assemble in the corridor. I kept my eyes closed and stayed in my bed, but Miria, whom I would come to know as a bully of the highest order, roused me. I joined the others in the corridor.

"Remove your clothes and start dancing," Bless ordered. Others obeyed her, but I stood still.

"Why are you not taking off your clothes?" Miria asked. "Do you think you are more special than these obedient girls?"

"Who are you to tell me to remove my clothes?" I asked. Someone slapped me so hard I staggered. "I am not going to take off my clothes,"

I insisted. "I won't dance naked." And then I issued a warning. "No one knows tomorrow, but I believe that you will pay for all the terrible things you do to other people."

Everyone stared. "Are you saying you will do something bad to me?" Miria asked.

"No. You are the one bringing terrible things upon yourself. Did you come here to study or to mistreat other girls? Imagine if someone was doing this to your sister. How would you feel? You may think there is a difference between us, but we are all human beings. I don't care whether you grew up in a town or a village, we are all here for an education. Hopefully, we understand that we are all equal."

And then I walked back to bed. I hid under my blanket and sobbed all night. I struggled to understand why opposition stood in my way after every breakthrough.

We woke up at four or five. At six we fetched water from the tap. If you were late to the faucet, you would miss your shower, and other students would mock you. As a junior student, I collected water for myself and for senior students. This water-collection hierarchy was a form of hazing or bullying, and if we didn't get their water, these bigger, stronger girls would beat us. They particularly picked on new students, students without siblings, and students who looked like they came from villages. I met all three criteria. Sometimes, they also made us wash their clothes.

After getting the water, I would do morning prep for an hour, which involved reviewing material from the previous day's classes. Then I would take my shower.

At seven, we headed to the school cafeteria for breakfast. We lined up to receive our plates of food; the senior girls would make us line up for their food as well as our own. We received a cup of corn-flour porridge mixed with hot water. We could take our breakfasts back to our dorm rooms if we wanted, but I always ate mine under the tree in the courtyard with my friends and classmates.

After breakfast we attended assembly. We'd line up by class, the students in senior one to four in grey skirts; the ones in senior five and six in black skirts; and all of us in crisp white dress shirts. Assembly was a time for the school administrators and teachers to relay important information: they'd call out the names of the students who were on the list for a beating, those who were being expelled, and those being sent home to get the money to pay their school fees. Monday assembly was the longest because so much happened over the weekend that had to be accounted for. On Fridays, for example, many students snuck out of school to get food. If that meant they missed Friday's roll call, they would be punished for it on Monday. Students who were called for a beating would have to go up in front of the whole school and, depending on how severe their transgression, receive five, ten, or fifteen strikes on the buttocks with a big stick.

Classes ran from eight until four with a one-hour break for lunch. My classes included chemistry, biology, physics, math, English, geography, commerce, and fine art. With the exception of two or three women, all the teachers were men. We were scared of them. It didn't seem to me that any of them thought of their profession as an act of service. They talked to us through beating us. If we arrived late or talked in class, the class monitors would report us, and the teachers would hit us. Mostly this was a smack across the head or the shoulders. Sometimes they'd force us to spend two or three hours of class time cleaning the compound. I quickly learned that my life was in their hands: even if I worked hard, if a teacher didn't like me, he could give me poor marks or hold me back a grade, and because I wasn't a girl from a wealthy family, I was unlikely to find favour with the teachers. I would later learn that male teachers posed another threat.

For lunch and dinner, we ate beans and corn flour cooked in a pan of boiling water. We were required to eat these meals in the courtyard. Most of the beans were infested; we commonly saw weevils floating in our meals. Some students went on hunger strikes in hopes of improving the menu, to no avail. Given my experiences since the war, the food didn't bother me.

That first term was not easy. After the first week, I despaired. I had heard that if you crushed radio batteries and ate them, you would die. I actually contemplated putting crushed batteries in water and drinking it. I was often lonely, and many times I wanted to quit. I fetched water, washed clothes, made beds, and cleaned the compound for the girls who ruled the roost. They targeted rural girls like me. The girls from the cities had luxuries like sugar, powdered milk, multiple pairs of shoes, and soft towels. They could sing all of Celine Dion's songs. They were respected. Village girls like me who did not know who Celine Dion was and had few belongings were always at risk. At least no one took my things. Seniors confiscated Betty's food, dresses, books, and pens. Other students found their shoes or towels dropped in the toilet or their books ruined. Another student warned us not to report anything to the school. The best way to survive was to keep quiet and be obedient.

I had hoped that because we had similar issues as girls, we would take care of each other and lift each other up. But that was not the case. I recalled my grandmother's story about a farmer who found a bunch of grasshoppers. He put them in a container, but they all struggled to get out, so he put a lid on the container. They immediately began fighting and eating one another. "You are fighting and eating each other when you know that I am going to crush you all in my mouth," the farmer said. "You better be nice to each other, because your ending is going to be the same!" Human beings, too, are so often against each other. When I think about the problems we face, they're all caused by people. What is the point of killing your neighbour or hating them when you know you're next in line? I just can't understand that. I believe our role is to take care of each other.

I also remembered everything I had endured, including hungry lions. I vowed to stand up for myself. I decided to pick my battles; I would continue to fetch water and line up for food, but I wouldn't obey anyone's more outrageous orders or put up with physical abuse. Despite the warnings not to say anything, I threatened to report the bullies. To my surprise, they yelled at me and asked me, "Who do you think you are?" but none of them slapped me, and no one tried to force me to dance naked ever again. My classmates came to see me as fearless.

Human needs are endless, and happiness comes only when you are satisfied with and grateful for what you have. I tried to focus on what I had instead of what I lacked, and I had so much in school: I ate three meals every day, slept on a mattress, showered twice a day, and was getting a secondary education at no cost. When I had a tough day, I consoled myself by reading. The first time I walked into the school library, the number of books on the shelves overwhelmed me. I vowed that I would read every single one. My knowledge would expand through reading, and I would succeed because of books. I was particularly drawn to feminist books and women's stories, but I didn't find very many of those. Most of the authors were men, and I was always asking myself, Where are the women? Where are their voices? They were mostly absent from our library's shelves.

I still had times when I felt lonely and felt like quitting. More than once I was keenly aware of my poverty relative to many of my classmates. Once I was invited to a party at the school, but I had no clothes to wear and couldn't find anyone with a dress to loan me. I ironed my uniform and went to the party in that. At the end of term, I would sometimes be the last to leave school because I did not have money for transportation home. My pocket money from the Windle Trust worked out to around twenty-five dollars per term, and I couldn't always make it last. Sometimes I'd be confident I had enough set aside to pay my fare home, only to find out that the fares had increased. And once I loaned money to a friend who promised to repay me before the end of term. When the time came, however, she didn't have any money. I would have been stuck at school had not one of the teachers helped me.

I tried very earnestly to be my own person on my own terms. But I knew this could cost me friends or supportive peers who could help me with my homework. And if I dug in my heels on every principle or value, I might miss out on the experience of working with a group toward a common goal. I tried to balance my instinct for independency and agency with my desire to develop myself socially and academically. So when my friends Anita, Donale, and Consulate decided to pierce their ears and asked me to join them, I said I would. I didn't want to disappoint them. That weekend, we bought a needle and sat under a tree. All of us wanted to wear earrings like city girls did, but nobody wanted to do the actual piercing. Anita asked me to do it because I was the bravest person in the group, but I couldn't stand the sight of blood. After a lot of back and forth, Anita finally said she would do it. She held Donale's ears and pushed the needle through the lobe while Donale screamed. Then she did Consulate. Every time Anita pierced an ear, I shut my eyes. Donale pierced Anita's ears, and then it was my turn.

"Can we do it after supper?" I asked.

"No!" Anita said. "We had a plan. You can't change your mind at the last minute. If you want to be a member of this group, you have to follow whatever we say."

"Girls, I love you, but there are things I can't do. I can't handle that amount of pain."

"You should have said that at the beginning!"

"It's okay if you can't accept me as your friend because I won't get my ears pierced," I told them. "I am willing to be your friend whenever you want. I am not afraid to be alone. If you believe being in this group means you can make me do anything, you are wrong."

But despite my brave words, I soon missed my friends. A few days later, I approached them after class. "I am willing to pierce my ears," I said, "but I prefer to do it in the salon. I heard that it doesn't hurt as much as using a needle." The next weekend, I paid five hundred shillings to have my ears pierced in a salon. One pop of the gun on each lobe, and the pain vanished almost immediately. We had to sit in the back of the class until our piercings healed. If a teacher discovered you had pierced your ears, they'd pull your lobes.

When the first term ended, I was excited to go home. I imagined my triumphant return. I planned to enter the village with a beautiful smile on my face so other girls would think secondary school was heaven. I'd keep the ugly part of the story to myself. With a joyous heart and a wide smile, I packed my clothes into a backpack I bought with my pocket money from Windle Trust instead of the case I'd brought with me. I knew the case would take up space in the taxi, which would cost more money.

When I arrived in the camp, I stood outside our tent in my freshly ironed white shirt with the straight collar, my white stockings, and my black shoes. I had used Medifair, the best lotion on the market, to make my skin beautiful. I wanted Mama to see how much I had changed. I wanted to show everyone how much I appreciated the opportunity to earn an education. I was shaking with anticipation.

And then a neighbour saw me and told me that my sister Godance had, like our sister Uwimpuhwe, married at sixteen, and my family had moved away. I felt like someone had punched me in the stomach. I stared at the tent for a long time. Then I dropped my backpack and my mattress and sank to the dirt, my head in my hands. What had I done to have suffered the loss of my family again? Had my father finally killed my mother? Was he in jail? I told myself that it was most likely that my mother had again fled his violence, but I had no idea where she and my siblings had gone. A million thoughts ran through my head. Where would I sleep for the two weeks until the next term of school started? If I could find a man who would marry me but allow me to go to school, I thought, I will say yes, but of course I didn't know any married women who attended secondary school.

I picked myself up and went to Murora's. She agreed I could stay with her as long as I helped with the chores. I worked in Murora's garden and developed callused palms and sore, bleeding nails, but I was used to this and decided to carry my cross and my burdens.

As the time to return to school approached, Murora started openly discouraging me from going back. She advised me to say goodbye to education and get married instead. "That's why your parents left you behind," she said. "They know you are a woman now, and you can take care of yourself."

Seeds of suspicion sprouted in my mind. I concluded that Murora planned to have me forcibly married to some man, perhaps to someone who agreed that I would keep working in her garden after he made me his wife. When the day came for me to return to school, I pretended to be too sick to work in the garden. As soon as Murora went out, I packed my backpack, rolled up my mattress, and walked the two hours to the trading centre, where I hired a taxi to take me back to school.

At school, I didn't tell anyone what had happened to me during the vacation. I pretended to be a girl from a happy home. I kept my uniform clean and pressed and always looked smart. I became known as one of the neatest girls in school.

ELEVEN

Lost and Found

One Friday, Molly, the school's registration officer, came to my classroom and announced that I had a visitor. Everyone stared. No one had ever come to visit me at school before. I was so sure Molly was mistaken that at first I didn't get up. Molly called my name again, impatiently, and I picked up my books and followed her.

I found my friend Leah waiting for me. We had lived in the same part of the camp and attended primary school together, but she was attending a different high school. We sat at a long table under a tree in the compound. Leah explained that she was on her way to Mbarara and stopped to deliver a message to me from my sister Godance.

Leah had bumped into Godance in the market. When Leah mentioned her upcoming trip, Godance said, "Please tell Kadur where I am and give her my address. I don't know how she is doing or where she went for the school break, and I am concerned about her. I heard rumours that she had dropped out of school."

I wept. "You have no idea of the joy in my heart," I told Leah through my sobs. For the second time in my life, I'd wondered if I would ever be reunited with anyone in my family, and now I had someone to go to in the holidays and could look forward to the end of the second term.

When the time for the next break came, I was excited and nervous. I tried to picture Godance as a married woman. I wondered if she had a baby. I remembered her telling me once that she wanted to marry a man

who was tall and brown, like Bosco, and I wondered what her husband
was like. I was eager to see her house. Would it be thatched with grass or
with iron sheets, like a rich person's house? I wished I had the money to
buy a book on parenting to give her as a gift.

It felt like I would never get to the address Leah gave me. When I
did, I found my sister sitting outside. She had no idea I was coming. I
ran to embrace her as tears of joy fell.

"Is this really you?" I sobbed. "Is this a dream, or am I seeing you
for real?" I did not want to let her go. I felt like I had when I finally saw
my family after the long journey from Tanzania. I saw a baby crawling.
When Godance told me it was her daughter, I picked her up. "I am your
second mother," I told her, although she was too little to understand.

Godance and her husband had a banana plantation, but I could see
that they were not well off. Their house had a roof made of thatched
banana branches, and it was so tiny that I wondered where I'd sleep. I
had my school mattress with me, and when I put it down, it filled the
space. I was dirty from the journey but couldn't take a bath because
Godance had no water.

I asked Godance about the rest of our family. Elijah was a teenager
now. He attended primary school intermittently and moved between
family members and friends. Our sister Uwimpuhwe was living in
Kyaka. Her first marriage had lasted only a year before she returned to
our parents, but when our father beat her, she left again. She said she
would rather jump from marriage to marriage than live with our father.
Now she had married again. Before I'd left for secondary school, Mama
told me Bosco had gone to Aunt Karuhanga, but Godance had no news
of him.

I met Godance's husband the next morning. I got up early, as was
my routine, and started sweeping outside. He was not like the man
Godance had once dreamed of marrying — he was darker than Bosco
and shorter than Godance — but he was happy to meet me. He admired
me for attending secondary school. Later, when Godance and I had time

to talk, she admitted that she had married only because our family was poor and she was trying to escape our father's abuse. I told her never to allow her husband to hit her. I said this even though I knew that she would have nowhere to go if he did.

My favourite part of staying with Godance was taking care of Kobusingye, her daughter. I adored her. Godance didn't want me to help with chores. I'd raised her, she said, and it was her turn to repay me. She wouldn't even let me weed the garden because she didn't want me to go back to school with callused hands and torn nails. I enjoyed running around in the banana plantation that surrounded the tiny house, I met Godance's sisters-in-law, and I spent time with the neighbour children. We'd sit under a mango tree in front of the house and play cards. I helped some of the girls to learn to read and write. I wanted to inspire them to go to school, too. One father told me he wanted his daughters to become nurses. He loved the crisp uniform and the white hat. But when I told him that my career would be something that would help me advocate for girls and women, he disapproved. He said no man would marry me because men only love women who respect them and don't criticize them.

The two weeks I stayed with Godance brought us closer than we had been before. We didn't talk a lot about our mother, and we didn't discuss what had happened until much later.

I had a persistent "admirer" at school, to my dismay. To make matters worse, he was the director of studies and also my geography teacher. Mr. Gilbert was forty-six and married with three kids. He would "joke" about making me his second wife when I finished secondary school. He'd often summon me after classes to ask me to help him carry his books and notebooks from the classroom to his office or residence. He chased other girls, too. All the students knew, but nobody reported him. What would be the point?

I first became aware of his attentions when I was nineteen and a senior two student. The senior four students who could pay fifty thousand shillings were going on a field trip to Kasese. Mr. Gilbert came into the dormitory and asked me if I was ready to go. I pointed out that not only did I not have fifty thousand shillings, but I wasn't a senior four student. He assured me the bus had space for me and told me to get ready. I was thrilled. I borrowed Anita's shoes and someone else's backpack because mine was getting old, packed my lotion and soap, and headed to the parking lot. When I got on the bus, all hell broke loose. "You're in senior two! You're not supposed to be here!" I heard someone shout, and from someone else, "Who cares if she paid her money?"

After that, the school administrators and teachers knew that Mr. Gilbert favoured me. Nobody spoke harshly to me for fear that I'd report them. The cafeteria workers gave me larger portions and even matooke, a food generally served only to students with health conditions. I enjoyed the privileges even though I suspected I would have to pay for them eventually.

I was taking a nap one Saturday evening when I received a message that he wanted to see me in his office. I dreaded what was going to happen, but I also knew I couldn't refuse to go. It took me fifteen minutes to make the one-minute walk from the dormitory.

"How are you?" he asked.

"I'm tired. My day was hectic, and I was getting some rest when I got your message."

"Do you mind if I take you out tonight?"

"To do what?"

"Kadur, do you know that I love you?"

My heart began to race. I prayed that someone would come to the office. He stood and grabbed my wrist. He was much taller and his height intimidated me. He forcefully kissed me as I cried and struggled. Then he promised that if I had sex with him, he'd reward me with good grades and the first position in his class.

A sudden knock on the door rescued me. He pushed me away and pretended nothing had happened. Anita came in to tell me that dinner was almost over and the kitchen would close soon. I made my escape. I headed straight to the dormitory while Anita brought my meal to me. I tried to eat, but the food kept getting stuck in my throat. I told Anita what had happened but asked her to keep it a secret. I passed a sleepless night, wondering when my struggles would end. Again I found myself thinking about suicide; this time I thought about hanging myself from a bush.

The next day, I avoided Mr. Gilbert like the plague and tried to make sure I was never alone. Anita volunteered to be my constant companion, especially if he summoned me to his office. Two days later, he called me to the office again. Anita came with me. When we went in, he told her to leave, but she went out to the veranda, where she could still hear us. When he realized she was within earshot and went to confront her, I made my escape again. A few weeks later, Anita went to get her hair cut without permission. He knew she had left the school and used this opportunity to call the roll. If you missed one roll call, they beat you. If you missed two, they'd suspend you for two weeks, and when you returned, you had to bring your parents with you; some students were then beaten by their parents in front of everybody. The third time you missed roll call, they'd expel you.

This was the first time Anita had missed a roll call, but we were sure that she'd be expelled. He wanted to take her out of the equation. We spent that evening talking over all the times we'd shared together at school, and she packed her clothes in preparation for her departure, certain that at the next day's assembly, they'd announce her expulsion. I felt responsible for Anita's persecution and so ashamed of what Mr. Gilbert was doing to me.

Assembly started with a prayer and then the national anthem. Then the headmaster stood to speak. "Where is Anita?" he asked. Fearfully, she raised her hand. "I want you to pack your stuff and leave. We had a roll call yesterday, and you were absent." Everyone was silent as Anita stood and left the assembly. I followed her. The matron challenged me, but I told her that Anita had some of my books in her suitcase and I needed to get them.

In the dormitory, I hugged Anita. I told her not to worry and promised that I would fight for her. Then I went to class. Through the window, I watched Anita leave the school with her mattress and luggage. I sobbed, and everyone else who loved her cried, too.

At the first opportunity, I went to see the headmaster, Mr. Kabikire. I asked him if Anita was expelled or just suspended for two weeks.

"It's an expulsion."

"I don't think that's fair. Can you check Anita's record and see if she has ever done anything wrong? We all know the process for getting expelled from this school, sir. Three other girls missed the roll call, too, and nobody said anything about them. Look at the list used by the teacher who called the roll. If the names of those girls are there, you can call me a liar."

The headmaster listened to me with a look of shock. "Do you want to go with her?" he asked. "I know that she is your best friend, but you don't have permission to barge into my office and spout nonsense!"

I insisted that I wanted him to explain why Anita was expelled and not the other girls who also missed the roll call, and why, if Anita had never missed roll call before, the school was punishing her with expulsion instead of the customary beating. He told me to leave his office, warning me that I would be in trouble if I didn't. I left, aware of the consequences of confronting the headmaster but knowing I would rather speak up than stay silent. It was Anita today, but it could be me or someone else tomorrow.

That evening, Mr. Kabikire summoned me, Kaneza, Denise, and Betty to his office. He wanted to see what Anita's other friends thought of her expulsion. As we waited outside, I asked them for their opinions. To my shock, they all thought Anita had gotten what she deserved. I pointed out that it was Anita's first offence. I argued that maybe we could change the way the teachers punished us. But when we went into the headmaster's office, they simply nodded in agreement with him. Later, I asked them why. They told me that I should have kept quiet lest I suffer Anita's fate. She was gone, and I should just focus on my studies.

I was too outraged to follow their advice. I was right, and I wanted to stand up for what I believed. I knew a girl whose father was on the school board. She gave me his phone number, and that weekend I called him. I told him everything, including exactly why Anita had become a scapegoat. He promised not to reveal my name when he talked to the headmaster. As I hung up the phone, a wave of panic churned my stomach. What had I done?

That Sunday evening, I did my nails and styled a friend's hair — anything to take my mind off what might happen next. As soon as the headmaster's car entered the school gates, girls deserted their boyfriends, students ran into their dormitories, and everyone pretended to study. I flung myself down on my bed.

He sent for me after dinner. I wasn't scared as I approached his office. My time had come; I was ready for anything. He asked me if I had a phone number for Anita. I said I could try to reach her. He told me to find a way to connect with her and tell her to return to school the next day.

I had Anita's sister's phone number. It took three tries before I reached Anita.

When Anita returned, the headmaster told her that she must never again leave school without permission, and the next time she missed roll call, she'd be expelled. I was so joyful to have successfully fought against her unfair expulsion. This was the first time in the school's history that an expelled student was allowed to return.

Unfortunately, I did not bring an end to Mr. Gilbert's sexual harassment. Once, when I was sick and asleep in the dormitory, I felt someone slip into bed next to me. At first I thought it must be Anita, but then I heard a man's voice whisper, "Kadur."

"Jesus!" I shouted. "Who are you?"

"Quiet, please!" I recognized Mr. Gilbert's voice, jumped out of bed, and fled. The next morning, I went to see him. I had decided to play along to buy myself time. I pleaded with him to be patient with me. I didn't want to become pregnant before the final-year exams, I said. After I graduated, I promised, we could meet somewhere outside of school. I was lying; I had no intention of giving in to him. I played along because I didn't want him to give me terrible grades. After the exams, I'd disappear, and I would go to a different school to do my A-levels.

I still had no idea where my parents were. It was halfway through my final term, and my friend Felesta's mother came to the school to see her. Parents who were able to do so often visited at the halfway point. Felesta introduced me to her mother, Josephine. As we talked, Josephine told me that she had lived in Kajaho Trading Centre in the Oruchinga Camp before moving to Kyaka, a refugee camp in the west, after a river flooded her land. Kyaka was a six-hour drive from where my parents had lived in Oruchinga. I wondered if they had done the same thing. Josephine asked me their names.

"My mother's name is Julian, and my father is Nkuranga."

"Really?" Her eyes widened. "They are my neighbours!" She wrote down the details so I could locate my parents when the term ended. I was so anxious to see Mama again.

I wrote my final exams and then left school as soon as I could. It felt good to be free of Mr. Gilbert's harassment, and soon the search for my family would be over. I missed my mother very much. I wondered if she assumed that I had already left school and gotten married. I clutched the paper with the address and a sketch of a map and my money in my trembling hands. I thought about keeping them in my bag, but if a thief stole my bag on the way, what would I do?

My trip would be a complicated one. I had to go from Isingiro to Mbarara to Kasese to Fort Portal to Kyegegwa and then to Bukere, a village in the Kyaka camp. I took a taxi to Mbarara and then hopped on a minibus going to Kasese. When we arrived, I gave the conductor the only bill I had — all my money — expecting he would give me change so I could pay the fare for the next leg of my journey. More than once I asked for my change. He told me to be patient and tossed down my things from the luggage place on the roof of the minibus. While I gathered them up, he vanished. I looked around, asking people if they'd seen him. People just stared at me blankly. In Kasese, they spoke Rukonjo, which was not a language I knew. I decided I would sell whatever I could, including my mattress, to get money for the rest of my fare.

I noticed a woman with a mobile call box, a wireless pay phone. People without phones of their own who needed to make calls paid her for its use. She was watching me. I approached her and she spoke to me in English. I explained my situation, and she seemed sympathetic. I showed her the map I had with me. She told me my destination was very far and asked how I planned to reach it. I suggested that she could buy my mattress from me or help me to find someone who would buy it.

"Your mattress is old," she said, "and the money I would give you wouldn't be enough to take you to Fort Portal."

Night was falling. I suddenly remembered a story I'd heard about how people in Kasese eat humans. The thought that I was stranded in an area of cannibals made my heart pound. When the woman was ready to close her kiosk for the day, I knelt before her and pleaded for her to take me to her house, promising to repay her even if it meant I had to live with her for months while I earned my fare home. My appeal moved her to tears. We squeezed my metal case into her kiosk. She made a phone call, and soon a boda boda, a taxi motorcycle, arrived.

I sat behind the driver, and the woman sat behind me. They chatted in Rukonjo, and because I could not understand them, I worried that they were plotting my death. For a few minutes, we flew through the night. When we stopped, I found myself in front of a row of attached houses. Happy children were playing outside, which reassured me. The woman paid for the trip and the biker left.

Her house was modest. Inside I saw a bed, a couch, some plates, and a few cooking pans. She changed her clothes and went out to a restaurant to buy a meal of rice, beans, and meat. I was famished. The meat tasted strange. I knew it was cow's skin. I left it and devoured the rice and beans. Then she gave me water for my bath and lotion for my skin. After I'd bathed, we untied my mattress, and she made my bed with an extra sheet she had. She was soon fast asleep, but I sat on the edge of the couch, too apprehensive to lie down. I was so exhausted that I nodded off in spite of myself, and I woke up only when the woman tapped me to ask me to sleep on my bed instead of her couch.

The next morning, the same biker picked us up and took us back downtown. The woman set up her kiosk. I sat down, unable to think of what to do next. When the woman asked me how I was going to get out of there, I burst into tears. She hugged me and then told me she'd pay the biker to take me to the police station. "Tell them your story, and I'm sure they will find a way to help you," she said. I thanked her for lodging me, copied down her phone number, and then the biker took me to the police station. I felt ashamed for feeling so suspicious of people who turned out to be my saviours just because of a story about cannibals I'd once heard.

The police were not so kind. I told my story, and the officer at the counter accused me of lying. "What kind of student are you when you don't even have a school uniform?" he asked. "We always encourage students who are returning home to wear their uniforms for easy identification."

School officials had warned us that men preyed on girls travelling alone and took them to motels to have sex with them, and they advised us to wear our uniforms when travelling. That way, if such a thing happened, someone would recognize us as a student and help us. I wasn't wearing my uniform because I wanted my shirt to be clean and white when I saw my mother again. I told the officer that someone at school had stolen it.

"Do you have anything to prove that you are a student? Which school are you from?"

Again, I lied. Thinking that my school was too remote for him to recognize the name, I told him Masheruka Girls, a well-known school in a big city. Of course, he immediately wanted me to name the headmaster. I had to pull out my books and answer questions about my subjects for him to believe that I was actually student.

"You are lucky," he said. "I thought that you've been in the city selling yourself, and now you want to go back home and don't have money, so you came here to get fake help."

He took me to the bus park, found a minibus, and ordered the driver to drop me at the bus park in Fort Portal. He told me to go the police station when I arrived and explain my situation, and they would help me.

I waited on that bus for hours, sleeping and waking and sleeping again, until the conductor had collected enough passengers for the bus to roar to life and leave. As we rumbled down the road, a gospel song from the bus's sound system filled the air. I recognized it at once: it was a song by a Ugandan gospel singer named Judith Babirye, and I thought the driver chose it just for me. She sang about needing Jesus to be with her in her time of struggle. The lines "Please don't leave me alone, Jesus, what I need is to be with you / Nobody knows about my situation, only you, God," could have come from my heart. I didn't want the song to end. I wondered what tough times Judith Babirye had endured. Everyone has a story. We all walk a path, and we all go through hard times. My path was harder to walk than most. I had seen things nobody had seen and suffered more than anybody should. Again and again, I had to overcome obstacles that blocked my way. I had moments of great doubt, but I believed that God was leading me to something greater. I was growing stronger in understanding and faith.

We reached Fort Portal early that evening. I was relieved to learn that most people spoke Rutoro, which was very close to Runyankore. The police station was so far from where the bus stopped that I had to hire a biker to take me. He asked for two thousand shillings. I didn't have a penny, so I lied and told him I would pay when we got to the station. All the way, I prayed that a police officer would come to my rescue. The biker would probably confiscate my belongings otherwise. When we arrived, he helped me unload my things and stood expectantly for his fare. I told him I couldn't pay him, and he started screaming. A police officer came out of the station, listened to my story, thanked the biker for helping me, and told him to return to the station later to get the fare.

One of the three officers in the station spoke English. He was tall and rotund with a moustache. I thought he must have been in his forties or fifties. Again, I said I had come from Masheruka Girls. He asked to see my student identity card, but I told him it had been stolen.

"I know the headmistress at Masheruka Girls," the officer said. "I'm going to call and ask if she knows you." So I told him the truth. When I finished, he asked, "Do you speak Runyankore?"

"Yes, sir."

"I'm from Ankore," he said in Runyankore. "And you're going to Kyegegwa?"

"Yes."

"Don't worry, you are home. I'll finish my shift in a few minutes. It's too late for you to get a bus to Kyegegwa. You'll have to wait until tomorrow morning. I'll tell my coworkers that you'll come home with me, and I'll put you on the bus tomorrow." He directed another officer to keep my things safe in the station for me. I was thrilled to meet someone who spoke my language. Because he spoke Runyankore, I felt I could trust him. It was the immediate bond you feel when you're somewhere unfamiliar and meet a stranger who speaks your language. That instant trust can land you in serious trouble.

He changed from his uniform into street clothes and we left the station. After we'd walked for about ten minutes, he suddenly put his arm around my waist and pulled me closer to him. "Your smile is killing me," he said. "I like girls with dimples." I had no idea what *dimples* meant, and I was too frightened to ask.

He led me into a restaurant and ordered me mashed banana with peanut soup, chicken, and a fruit-flavoured soft drink called Mirinda. The restaurant was quiet and we were the last customers of the day. We sat in a corner and ate. Then the police officer left. When I'd finished my meal, a woman who worked in the restaurant asked me to follow her. She led me behind the building to a lodge. When she opened the door, the police officer joined me. The woman left us.

"This is where you'll sleep tonight," he said. "This is your key. Everything you need is inside. If you need to take a shower, the girls will show you the bathroom and towel. Do you know you are beautiful?"

"Not really," I said.

"I think I'm going to spend the night with you." He told me to sit on the bed. I was surprised; I'd thought he'd gotten this room for me to sleep in, that he would leave and come back for me in the morning. He stood before me, telling me how he would provide for all my needs and send me money at any time, but I barely heard him. My mind was racing, trying to think of how I could get him to reconsider. How could a respected man, a police officer old enough to be my father, dare to do such a thing? I had come to the police for help, and he saw it as an opportunity to have sex with me. I remembered the song I'd heard on the bus. If God is with me, I told myself, he won't allow this police officer to rape me.

"Look at your hands and mine," I said with a trembling voice. "We are different. I came to the police station because I thought that you would help me. Listen to what you are telling me. You can force me to do what you want, but rest assured that you will never get away with this. When I get my belongings from the station tomorrow, I will report you to your colleagues. I am a student and not a street girl. You might have done this to other girls and got away with it, but today will be your last day as a police officer." Of course, I had no idea what would happen if I reported him. His fellow officers might shrug off my report. Perhaps they'd think that because I had gone with him and accepted a meal and lodging from him, I owed him whatever he wanted.

He stared at me in amazement. Finally he said, "It looks like I've wasted my money today. I paid for the food and lodge. When you finish school, you'll have to pay that back."

"But you didn't ask me if I was interested in having sex with you. You assumed I would agree. You are a respected man, but not everyone will say yes to you. Most girls are afraid of you and what you might do, but I have been through too much to fear you."

He got to his feet. "Let's go," he said. "I'm taking you home." He returned the key to the lodging keeper. As we walked to his house, he said, "I have a wife and kids. Please don't say anything to my wife. Pretend as if nothing happened."

At his house, his wife opened the door. She welcomed us, and I felt safe. The police officer explained that I'd come to the station very late and was hungry, so he'd taken me to a restaurant to eat. She offered me tea, which I declined. She prepared a bed for me. I slept like a dead body on the six-inch-thick mattress — so much better than the two-inch one I had for school!

When she woke me up the next morning, he had already gone to work. Their children, some of whom looked to be my age, were excited to meet the stranger who'd spent the night. They hugged me and chatted in Runyankore as they prepared for school. The bus to Kyegegwa left early, so I ate my breakfast quickly. She summoned a biker to take me back to the police station to get my things.

At the station, the biker loaded my belongings and drove me to the bus while a different officer followed on his own motorcycle. The bus was almost full, but the police officer spoke with the driver, who agreed to drop me off at Kyegegwa. Before he left, the officer gave me his phone number and told me to call him when I reached home. Then he started flirting with me. I could not wait for the bus to leave.

At Kyegegwa, I found a biker to take me to Bukere. This time, I told him that I didn't have any money myself but that someone would pay him when we arrived. The ride lasted for almost forty minutes. Thick forest lined both sides of the road. The biker told me that many people lived in the area, primarily refugees from Congo and a few Rwandans. I began to see fewer trees and more houses. The biker stopped at a busy place where people were working and selling food and supplies. This was the trading centre in Bukere, the biker told me, and it was as far as he would take me. I began to panic. I feared that he would beat me and take my belongings, leaving me stranded with no money and nothing to trade. And then I saw someone I knew: Mugabo, my sister's former husband from Oruchinga. I had no idea he had also relocated to Kyaka.

I greeted him and asked for his help, promising that either I would pay him back or my mother would. He pulled money from his pocket and asked how much I needed. After he'd paid the fare, I asked him if he knew where my family was. "I do," he said, "but you will have to get another motorcycle." We couldn't find a biker who was going in the right direction, so Mugabo said he would take me. He had a bicycle and attached my things to it. I walked closely behind him as he slowly pedalled. Many times he got off the bike and pushed it, especially up the hills. Eventually the road disappeared.

It was the rainy season, so the plants were green and blossoming. You could tell by the size of the cones on the trees that the soil was very fertile. The grasses were tall, and the flies were thick. Over and over

I asked Mugabo if we were almost there. Every time I saw a house, I thought it was my mother's. Mugabo wanted to surprise me, so when we did reach the right house, he said nothing.

Elijah saw me first. He ran and jumped on me, and we both tumbled to the ground. He was a grown-up boy — even his voice had changed! He told me that Mama was at a friend's house. I wanted to surprise her, so I hid behind a tree while Elijah fetched her. When he returned with her I heard her say, "Stop lying to me. You can play these games with your friends but not me."

I crept up to her from behind, and then I embraced her. When she turned and saw my face, we clung to each other. Neither of us could speak. I opened my mouth, but I had no words. Only tears.

TWELVE

The Long Road Home

It had been three years since I'd last seen my mother. I talked about school, about how I had finished senior four and was waiting for the results of my national exams. I told her to keep her fingers crossed for me. I didn't care if I didn't do my A-levels, but I wanted good grades for senior four. It mattered to me to do well. I wanted the Windle Trust to know that I had not wasted its money, and I wanted to prove to people who thought that girls or children from poor families didn't deserve an education that I could endure hardship and my hard work was paying off. I didn't tell her about Mr. Gilbert, or the times I'd felt so lonely and miserable that I'd thought about suicide, or the difficulties I'd had on my journey to Kyaka. I wanted her to believe that all was good with me.

I also told her that I had stayed with Godance on my last vacation. My family, of course, had no way of keeping in touch with Godance and had no idea how she was doing. I knew that Godance might have been expecting me to come to her again, and I felt terrible that I couldn't tell her I was going to Mama's. Godance didn't have a phone, and I didn't know anyone near her who had one. Connecting with someone in rural Uganda was rarely easy. People in cities and towns might learn of the death of a loved one if it were announced on the radio, but not everyone had a radio or the money to pay for a radio announcement, and radio broadcasts did not reach remote villages.

Life in Kyaka was more pleasant than in Oruchinga. The house was doorless and made with grass walls and a thatched roof, but we had plenty of food, and Mama's gardens overflowed with mangoes, oranges, and pawpaw. The only common fruit she didn't grow was avocado. There were large numbers of refugees pouring into Kyaka Camp from Congo. Congo has been at war for almost twenty-eight years, and it is hard to hope that peace will ever come. Countless people have perished. Congo is well-known as a nation of gold, which every country wants. Every ounce of gold extracted for the benefit of other nations, including the United States, is soaked in the blood of innocent Congolese.

My three younger brothers and my younger sister Sharitina were living with Mama. My father wasn't there, which didn't matter to me. I wouldn't have been happy or excited to see him, and he didn't care whether I came home or not. If he had been there, I probably would have had to sleep outside the house, and because there were no neighbours close by, it would have been very unsafe. At night if someone had to go outside to use the toilet, everyone else went outside with them because it wasn't safe to be out in the dark alone.

I went to the trading centre to buy soap one quiet Friday evening and happened across a meeting. A short, dark-skinned man was leading it, but he was struggling with Kinyabwisha, one of the languages the Congolese people speak, especially those from Masisi. It's similar to Kinyarwanda, but the words are archaic.

"Is there anyone who knows how to speak some English?" he asked in frustration. I raised my hand.

"I'm not really fluent," I said, "but I can communicate."

"Which other languages do you speak?"

"Kinyarwanda, Runyankore, Rukiga, and some Swahili."

"I'm going to speak to you in English, and you translate to Kinyabwisha."

That was how I met Jimmy. He was a UNHCR representative trying to tell the Congolese that refugee verification would soon commence. As I interpreted for him, he seemed to me a kind person with genuine concern and affection for the refugees. He smiled as, through me, he answered their questions. At the end of the meeting, I stayed and chatted with him. I told him that I had just finished senior four, which impressed him. He urged me to come to the local primary school on Monday to help interpret during the refugee verification process. He especially wanted me to help with the refugee girls. I could have hugged him.

I sprinted home, giddy with excitement. "I got a job," I gasped between laboured breaths.

"What kind of job?" Mama asked.

"I'll be working as an interpreter during the refugee verification." Elijah immediately wanted to know how much they'd pay me. "I don't care how much," I said. "What matters is that I am going to work, and the money I get will help us."

The next day I washed my clothes at the well in anticipation of Monday morning. I borrowed some money from a friend I'd made and used it to buy myself some face lotion and lipstick. I saw myself on a new level. At last I would enjoy the fruits of my sweat and tears. I had ample experience working hard to help my family, but this would be my first taste of using my education in my quest for independence. On Monday, I styled my hair, smoothed the lotion on my face, and applied my new lipstick. I didn't want to work for the United Nations looking like a pauper! I arrived at the primary school early to help set up outside and in the classrooms.

"What are you doing here?" a stern-looking woman asked me. I explained I'd been asked to come and interpret. "I don't know you," the woman said. "I know all the girls from this settlement but not you. Your name is not on the list I have with me." I felt my face flush. "Go and stand with the other refugees," she said, "and don't enter any of these offices except when someone tells you to come in."

I looked for Jimmy but he was nowhere in sight, and when I asked other workers if they'd seen him, they looked at me in puzzlement, as though they had no idea to whom I referred. Finally, a white car with the UNHCR logo drove up with Jimmy in the front seat. I waved when I saw him. He didn't recognize me with my new hairstyle and lipstick, but I introduced myself and told him what had happened with the stern woman. Together we went to her office. Her name was Emerida.

"We need only people who live here," Emerida said. "Not everyone can just come, enter this place, and start working."

Jimmy explained that he'd invited me because I'd helped him on Friday. I was a student, he said, and he wanted to give me the chance to earn some money for school supplies.

"Does she speak Swahili?"

"Not fluently, but most people here that we will be working with this week speak Kinyabwisha and Kinyarwanda."

"We have enough translators," Emerida insisted.

Jimmy's expression grew stern. "Emerida, she's going to work here. I have the right to stop any of your scheduled workers and recruit a new person." With that, he beckoned me to sign some papers, and I got to work. For the next three days, I kept people in line and ensured that older adults took priority. I earned five thousand shillings each day, which was an enormous sum for someone my age.

The verification centre moved to the refugee zone in Sweswe, and this time, I interpreted. When people who spoke Swahili made inquiries, the computer operator, who was fluent in Swahili, came to my rescue.

I had never heard of or seen a computer and at first didn't understand the difference between a computer and a television. I was utterly intrigued. When a family registered, the operator typed all their information into the computer. He also used the computer to take their pictures, and then he told them to press their fingers on a flat plate. It turned red when they put their hands on it, and at first I thought it would burn them. I learned later that it was a scanner that captured their fingerprints. Once the family was registered, another machine next to the computer printed out a piece of paper with all the information on it. At lunchtime, the operator used the computer to play music. How? I didn't ask questions because I didn't want to look stupid. I concluded the whole thing was magic. Most of the workers operated the computers like it was a normal thing to do, but they were university students. Suddenly I reconsidered my indifference toward further education. More worlds were out there that I could unlock. Education was the key.

The computer operator had a cellular phone and told me I could use it any time I wanted. I knew Anita's sister's phone number, so one evening I called her. I told her about my job and how much money I was earning. She was astonished. We talked for almost two minutes, and I gave her the number of my colleague's phone and told her she could reach me between eight and four. A week later, she called to tell me that the exam results were out. Not only had I passed, but the Windle Trust was willing to sponsor my A-levels. Betty had also made it but sadly Anita had not. I told Jimmy that I would have to stop working. I thanked him for the opportunity and for watching over me. My first real job had lasted only a month, but I knew it would inspire me for the rest of my life.

Mama had saved my earnings for me, but although it seemed like an impressive sum, it wasn't enough to pay for everything I'd need, and I also needed to pay for my transportation back to Mbarara and my new school. I needed a new mattress, a new bag, and books and stationery. I also needed a piece of luggage. The metal case was too heavy and awkward to place on motorcycles. Schools forbade radios, but I spent 7,500 shillings to buy one. The radio would allow me to keep track of what was happening in the world, and I couldn't imagine life without hearing the rich, vibrant voice of my favourite DJ, DJ Agnes. The songs she played had a way of making me forget my worries, and because she was a woman on the radio, she proved that women weren't solely for raising children and catering to men. I also admired Wandira Kazibwe, the vice president of Uganda and the first African woman to hold such a position.

The bus left Bukere at around four in the morning, and Bukere was a two-hour walk from my mother's house. A cousin of mine, Scovia, lived in Bukere, so I would spend the night with her.

When I reached Scovia's, she was preparing cabbage and rice for dinner. I helped cut the cabbage. As we were working, a young man, a friend of Scovia, dropped by. His name was Omar, and he was twenty-six. He had a beautiful smile. He was wearing open-toed shoes and had a natural gap between his two front teeth. I had always found men with a gap between their teeth handsome. When Omar learned that I was leaving for school the next day, he asked if I'd take his phone number.

"Yes, but I don't have a phone. How will I call you?"

"If you get a phone at school, I'll call you," he said.

After he left, Scovia told me that Omar was a God-fearing and humble man who did not drink. I didn't care about the God-fearing part; I knew many people who attended church faithfully but few true Christians. That he didn't drink was a point in his favour: I knew that if I did marry one day, it would not be to a man who drank.

But I wanted to stay focused on my future. I had known girls who lost their scholarships because they got pregnant at school, and even some who had lost their lives. If your boyfriend impregnated you, he'd likely deny it. Many girls in that situation turned to abortion. They'd buy herbs from a traditional herbalist in the hopes of inducing a miscarriage, and sometimes it killed them. Nobody talked about it.

The tiny houses being close to each other had exposed me to my neighbours' sexual lives. We heard everything. But because nobody talked about sex, I grew up thinking it was something that only married people did. When I got older, my girlfriends and I would talk about our experiences hearing our parents and neighbours, and when my labia were pulled, I knew it was to make me pleasing to my future husband. Nobody encouraged birth control, either, because girls weren't supposed to have sex before marriage. People would tell us, "If you use a condom, it will go inside your belly, and a few days later, you will burst," and if you bought condoms anyway and someone found out, then the whole village would know. Similarly, if you summoned up the courage to ask for birth control pills, the nurse at the clinic would tell everyone that you were sexually active. Stigmatizing contraception to prevent sexual relations has had disastrous consequences in Africa. The high birth rate has worsened the poverty in which so many Africans live, and AIDS has ravaged the population. By 2000, more than twenty-five million people in Sub-Saharan Africa were infected and hundreds of thousands had died, creating a generation of orphans.

For all my reservations, I couldn't help feeling attracted to Omar and pleased that he wanted to keep in touch with me. I could see a problem in the offing, however: he was Congolese, and as far as I knew, Congolese ate rats.

The journey to Mbarara took only four hours on a single bus. I felt embarrassed when I remembered what I'd gone through on the previous trip. If only I had known that one bus would take me the whole way!

My new school was Nyamitanga Secondary School. It was close to the Rwizi River, Mbarara Hospital, and Mbarara University of Science and Technology. It was a Muslim school, and I was nervous about how they treated Christian students. Should I wear a veil? Would they allow me to wear my short skirts or tell me to buy long ones? Would the students in the higher levels bully the new students?

A border of shrubs lined the front of the school. Barbed wire was on the gate at the main entrance. This was a co-educational school that offered O-level classes, which I'd already completed, and also A-levels. It would take two years to complete my A-levels. For the first year, I'd be a senior five student. You could distinguish the two groups by the uniforms they wore. O-level students wore light blue, and A-level wore light grey. The girls' skirts were long, and the Muslim girls sometimes wore the hijab.

I reported to the deputy headmaster. The school had two dormitories for girls, and I was assigned to Kuppa House. I learned that I wouldn't need to wear a veil or hijab, but that I was lacking in some essential school supplies that many of my dorm mates had brought with them, like sugar, powdered milk, extra shoes, and hardcover books that many of my dorm mates had brought with them. Betty had yet to arrive, but I spotted another girl from Isingiro Secondary School, Stella. She was a good Christian girl from Nakivale refugee camp and was also sponsored by Windle Trust, and we quickly became best friends. She was already settled in the dormitory but in a section without any empty bunks. To my relief, she told me that no one bullied the senior five students.

My goal was to work hard for the next two years. It was rumoured that Windle Trust would select one a female student from Oruchinga for a university scholarship. It was between me and Betty. I knew I would have to work hard to win it, but if I didn't, I expected I would return home and, in the absence of other options, perhaps get married. I was twenty-two and one of the oldest female students, but physically I was small. Nyamitanga wasn't a prestigious school, but it was close to the city, and so most of the students were from the city and some even attended as day scholars, returning home each day. City girls were perceived as completely different from rural girls. We thought they were well-to-do and didn't know how to cook, clean, or wash clothes because they had servants. Omar assumed I was a city girl because I was attending high school in the city, looked clean, and spoke English. He wondered if I knew how to take care of a house. His friends discouraged him from pursuing me because they also perceived me as a city girl and concluded I was incapable of being a "good woman."

Because I was generally kind and helpful, the school appointed me defence prefect, Mama Dormitory, aka Mama Dorm. This required me to settle disputes between students and to punish rule-breakers. As captain for Kuppa House, I was responsible for everything in the dorm, and Kuppa House was known as dirty and full of reckless, poorly behaved girls. I took my responsibilities seriously. I saw this as my opportunity to prevent the more senior O-level girls from bullying the lower students. But no one had ever successfully managed the tough girls in Kuppa House. "You're from a village," people said, "and those city girls will never listen to you." They feared no one, not even the teachers. At night, they'd sneak out and return in the morning, and if anyone reported them, they'd get beaten.

The first ten days felt like ten years, and I wanted to quit. But if reporting them wouldn't work, maybe talking to them would. Instead of reprimanding, punishing, and threatening girls who misbehaved, I encouraged them to focus on their studies. I knew that many of them snuck out at night to meet men; the school's monthly medical checkups quickly identified those who were pregnant, which meant instant expulsion. I told them that it broke my heart to see girls forced out of school because of pregnancy while the boys who impregnated them stayed in school. I challenged the girls to stand on their own and demand a better future for themselves.

Of course, it wasn't just off campus that female students could get into trouble. As in my secondary school, I quickly learned that male teachers did not hesitate to make advances to students, including me. They'd call you from your classroom and urge you to go out with them on the weekend. I'd almost lost count of how many men had tried to coerce or force me into having sex with them, including men in positions of authority and respect, who should have been trustworthy.

When I told my friend Byamukama about a teacher, Buwembo, who was pestering me to go out with him, he said he would tell the teacher that if he didn't stop, Byamukama would report him to the headmaster. That night, Byamukama stayed with me when the teacher tried to draw me into the office with him, and I was able to return to class unharmed. I appreciated that Byamukama cared enough to stand up for my rights, but I really didn't need anyone to protect me. After all I'd been through, I felt fearless. Since I had watched so many women coerced into relationships, I was very vocal that if a man tried to force me into marriage, I would leave. Even in primary school I would vow to poison the food of any man who forced me into a relationship. People said of me, "That girl is dangerous." Being thought of as too much trouble to bother with was fine with me.

More than once I had to deal with male teachers who tried to coerce me. Sometimes it worked if I just played along, putting them off until the end of term or a school year and then leaving as unobtrusively as I could so they wouldn't realize I had no intention of meeting with them. Other times, I had to talk about my right to determine what happened to my body and threaten to report them to the police, even though I knew from experience that police officers could also be sexual predators. Men were so unused to women standing up to them that my strong words worked.

At the end of the first term, Kuppa House was one of the cleanest, thanks to my ability to get the students to do their part, and the number of girls expelled for pregnancy had drastically declined. Unfortunately, my extra duties meant I had a lot on my plate, and my academic performance disappointed me. At the end of the first term, Betty placed third, and I came eighth.

By the end of the second term, I was known in the school as a positive influence on my peers. Some wondered how I had convinced the tough girls in Kuppa House to change their ways. My strategy was simple: I spoke with them openly and I led by example. I treated them with respect, and they grew to respect me and themselves. The administrators were so pleased with the transformation in my dormitory that they gave me money for a dorm party. Many respected teachers attended, and I felt like a queen surrounded by amazing women.

I returned to Kyaka at the end of the third term, and Omar soon became one of my closest friends. I'd tell my parents that I was going to see Scovia, but instead I went to Omar's house. At least twice a week I'd walk for an hour to visit him. I was not interested in a romantic relationship because I wanted to focus on my studies, but I liked talking with him. He cooked delicious meals for me, like eggs and rice — and to my relief I learned that he never ate rat. I wanted to show off my cooking skills for him, but he would not allow me to either cook or help with any household chores. He treated me like a city girl.

Even though Omar is from Congo and I am from Rwanda, we basically share the same culture. When I first met him, Omar presented himself as a devout Christian who regularly attended church and read the Bible. He would usually cook for me or collect the water. He seemed like a really good person: loving, caring, and helpful. He was such a stark contrast to my father. Many things about Omar have changed since the days of our courtship, but he is still very helpful around the house, which is uncharacteristic of the African men I know. After I'd met him four times, he asked to see my family home. When he visited, my parents didn't pay a lot of attention to him or ask about him. They thought he was just a schoolmate. But Omar could see that even though we lived in a mud house, I kept it very clean. Soon after that I visited his house for the first time and saw that he, too, was a very clean person. He had a garden with matooke, cassava, and corn. He gave me the impression that, unlike so many men in the camp who were idle and depended entirely on the aid they received, he was a very active man who provided for himself. But my education remained my priority, and I was still confident that I did not want marriage and children.

My friend Anita was an example of how women could suffer a lifetime of challenges after mixing with men. I had tried to contact her through her sister many times since I arrived at Nyamitanga, but the phone number was out of service. Then one day I was in town purchasing school supplies and a woman with a familiar face walked into the store. She was carrying something on her head and a baby girl on her back. When she saw me, she turned her face away. She was barefoot, and her feet resembled Anita's, so I approached her. She had her back to me, but I said, "How are you, Anita?" She turned and looked at me with eyes misty with tears.

"Kadur, I'm sorry," she said. "I wanted to speak with you, but I couldn't bear the shame."

"What happened to you?" I asked.

"After school, I got pregnant. When my sister found out, she asked me to leave her house. I had nowhere else to go, so I sold my mattress and settled here in Mbarara. The only job I could get was as a house girl, so I could have a place for myself and my child and food to eat." As she spoke, I began to cry. "I knew you were in Nyamitanga," she said, "but I didn't want you to know about any of this."

Anita was four months pregnant when she started working as a house girl. The man who impregnated her just disappeared; he had that freedom. Had Anita tried to claim him as the father of her child, he could easily have said, "I've seen you with a bunch of guys. This child isn't mine." When Anita's daughter, Winnie, was born, she never knew her father. This is ikinyandaro, which roughly translates to a child born to an unmarried woman who still lives with her parents. Young Christian women who got pregnant outside marriage could be rejected by their congregation.

Now Anita woke up each morning at five, made breakfast for four children, and prepared their parents' clothes for the day. After she took the children to school, she made the beds, washed the clothes, cleaned the house, and shopped for food. She prepared lunch and later dinner. I felt terrible for her. Again I wanted to use my voice to make things better for Uganda's women and girls. It was so cruel and unfair that

Anita would forever pay the price for giving in to temptation while the man who impregnated her faced no consequences.

Omar did once pressure me to sleep with him. I was making the trip from school to home and expecting to spend the night with Scovia before continuing to my parents' house the next day. She wasn't home. I didn't want to hire a biker to drive me to my parents' house because it was after dark and the soggy road would prolong the trip. I decided to walk to Omar's. I was apprehensive: I knew he had only one bed, and I wondered how I'd sleep in the same house with him. I was determined not to give in to temptation; I'd stick to my values.

Omar was still awake and listening to his favourite radio program. People in the camp often stayed up after dark, socializing. They didn't have much else to do. He was happy to see me when I knocked on his door. I explained my situation. Omar hugged me tightly.

"Are you sleeping here?" he asked.

"Yes, if you don't mind."

His smile grew as wide as the sun.

He offered me some leftover potatoes mixed with beans. It was still warm. I was hungry, but I didn't want Omar to know how much I loved to eat. Girls at school said they wouldn't eat a lot around boys because they didn't want to get a reputation for gluttony. Men found women who ate a lot unattractive. There was a saying, "Azakurira munzu" — "Women who eat too much will eat their husband." Boys and men, of course, could eat as much as they liked.

After I ate, I unrolled my mattress on the floor near his bed and took a shower. We talked a little bit, but I struggled to stay awake. I lay down on my mattress and fell asleep. A few hours later, his voice woke me up. At first I didn't remember that I was at Omar's. Then I heard him telling me to come and sleep in his bed. I was shocked. I told him that I would take my mattress and my blanket and sleep outside. I had done that many times when my father turned me out, and I could do it again. I got up and went into the kitchen. Omar followed me. He kept repeating that he couldn't sleep with me in the house as though I were his sister. I started to collect my things.

"I won't allow anybody to play with me," I told him. "This is the last time I'll be talking to you. I trusted you, and if I knew that you were going to turn against me like this, I wouldn't have come to your house."

I slammed the door behind me as I left. He followed me, apologizing profusely. Eventually I agreed to go back in, but my hands were shaking. I lay on my mattress, but I couldn't get back to sleep. I stayed awake for the rest of the night. I left early the next morning without saying a word to him, and for the rest of the vacation, I stayed away. I returned to school without saying goodbye. For three months, we didn't speak to each other. But on my next vacation, I met with him. He apologized to me for what had happened, and I forgave him. He did not pressure me after that, and I knew that I could trust him. I went to his house often, and he even gave me a set of keys.

Before I returned to school, Omar gave me his phone. It was a Samsung, a rare thing to have in the camp at that time. Students weren't supposed to have phones, but many snuck them in. I didn't have to contravene the school rules. Because of my track record as a competent leader and responsible young woman, the school allowed me to keep the phone. I had other privileges, too, such as mashed bananas and milk with my porridge. The recognition made me feel good. Some of my fellow students were happy that I had the phone because I let them use it to contact their friends and parents.

At the end of the year, the school organized a special party for the student leaders. I received many gifts from the teachers and the headmaster, including a fluffy and luxurious green towel like the ones I'd seen at the beach and a Thermos, in recognition of my impact on the female students. Everyone wished me good luck, perhaps thinking that I wouldn't return for senior six. I did, but during the vacation after the first term, Omar told me he loved me.

Omar often dwelled on the fact that I wasn't a Seventh-day Adventist like him. Seventh-day Adventists usually marry within their faith, and most Seventh-day Adventist women wear long skirts and don't have ear piercings. Despite this issue, Omar told me that he'd grown to love my personality and disposition. He didn't know much about my background, my family, or what I'd gone through, but I didn't mind that he didn't ask me a lot of questions about my past. I didn't want to talk about my trauma or be judged for what I went through. Omar focused on my present. He paid attention to my interactions with high-profile men, such as Henry, who worked at UNHCR, and liked that I was not tempted by them, expecting them to provide for me. That I was an independent person who could provide for myself impressed him. He also liked that I was very clean. I washed my clothes with fervour and dyed my hair, which made it look clean. Cleanliness was so important to Omar that before we met, he'd told Scovia how much he admired the way she took care of her house and asked her if she knew anyone who could care for a home the way she did, and Scovia told him about me. Our first meeting at Scovia's was not by chance.

Omar told me that he had fallen in love with the way I was in the world, and I realized that I was interested in him, too. He also told me that he'd recently made a refugee application to Canada.

Anyone who was a refugee could apply for resettlement in another country, but the process was not easy and often took many years. The war had displaced hundreds of thousands of people, and many waited in the queue to emigrate. Some would never get the chance. Canada was widely considered the best country in which to live. People viewed it as peaceful, stable, and secure, with less racism than places like the United States. For survivors of a war fuelled by cultural racism, those characteristics were very appealing.

Omar's life was in jeopardy in the camp (like me, Omar is reluctant to talk about some of his more painful experiences, so I do not know the details). This allowed him to file an application as a high-risk refugee, and when he was called for an interview he mentioned that he had a girlfriend and gave them my name. (I don't think he wanted to marry me just to make his refugee application stronger; our marriage ended up delaying his application for an extra year and a half.) He encouraged me to think about applying to get status in Kyaka because all my information was still in Oruchinga, but I worried that moving my file to Kyaka would affect my scholarship, and I wanted to finish my A-levels. I also loathed the idea of living in a Western country. I could not forget what had happened to my paternal grandmother when she followed her husband to Belgium, and I had also come to understand that leaders from Western countries had provided military aid to certain coalitions in Africa, even though they knew it would lead to civil war. They fanned the flames and then stood and watched as countless people were butchered like cattle. When I thought of the West, I could only picture hostility and hatred toward Africans. I told Omar to go to Canada alone, but he said he couldn't go anywhere without me. His friends thought he was crazy to give up the chance to live in Canada just because of a woman.

The months went by, and the end of my second year of A-levels drew near. I was preparing for my final examinations when the immigration office in Kampala invited Omar to come for an interview and asked that he bring me. I couldn't possibly leave school and make it to Kampala. He went alone, but they sent him away when he showed up without me.

When I returned to Kyaka, I promised to give Omar's words about marrying me serious consideration. I had written my A-level exams, and in the unlikely event that I secured a place in university and received a scholarship, I could attend as a married woman. Omar treated me like a queen. He loved me in a way that changed how I felt about marriage. We talked about what our journey as husband and wife could be like. I did not want to share with him everything I'd endured growing up, but I told him that I knew that I couldn't take what I'd seen Mama go through.

I had always been afraid of marriage, and yet the idea of marrying Omar made me happy. I realized that I wanted to have children of my own, and I knew I would be a good mother. I told Omar that I had never been in a romantic relationship with anyone, that I had hardened my heart against men because of the trauma I'd experienced. I'd grown used to assuming that every man I met would do me harm. But I knew that I loved him from the bottom of my heart, and so I gave my heart to Omar.

THIRTEEN
Married Life

My father did not make it easy for us. My parents had lofty expectations. My father had done everything he could to keep me from attending school, but now that I was the most educated girl in my village, he was keen to profit from my higher worth and anticipated receiving many cows in exchange for me. I knew that Omar could not afford even a single cow. I'd always found the practice of paying a dowry for a bride objectionable. I was not property for sale in a market. The idea that as soon as a man paid money or cows for me meant I would belong to him violated all my principles. I knew the practice began as a show of respect for the parents and a demonstration of how much the man valued his prospective wife, but I wanted to be free. I also didn't want the burden of having to repay the dowry if the marriage broke down.

At the UNHCR I was sometimes invited to interpret for refugees. This was how I met a respected protection officer, Henry Kiiza, who screened refugees seeking settlement in other countries and needed me to interpret for him. He did not hide that he was interested in me. He'd often ask me to go to lunch with him and would call me to his office and ask me to organize his files. Most people who wanted to see him had to make an appointment; he made it clear that I was free to visit him any time. I heard people muttering in the corners, asking why I was allowed to spend so much time in his office. Because of Henry's position, Omar cautioned me not to say anything about our engagement. "That guy has all the power to stop me from going to Canada if he finds out you are my girlfriend," he said. "If he asks me about you, I'll just say you are my sister." I was once walking with Omar when Henry pulled up in his car. He asked me how I was and then asked me about Omar. I told him Omar was my brother.

One evening when the offices were closing, Henry handed me some books he wanted me to take to his house. He gave me his keys and told me to put the books on a table near his bedroom and come back to the office. I felt I had to do as he asked. I phoned Omar to tell him what I was doing, and he told me to stay on the line with him. At Henry's, my phone in my hand, I unlocked the door and went inside. I put the books down on the table. That's when I heard footsteps, and Henry came into the house and crept up behind me. I tried to get past him, but he grabbed my wrists. Immediately I started to cry, but Henry didn't care. He was tall and strong, and he tried to push me to the floor. That was when Omar raised his voice, and Henry, startled, let go of me and asked who was on the phone. I said it was my father. Henry got very quiet. In Kinyarwanda, which I knew Henry could not speak, I told Omar that I thought Henry was going to rape me. While Henry kept asking, "What are you saying? What are you talking about?" I made it to the door and left. Later, I pretended nothing had happened. I kept going to Henry's office when required and talked to him as usual. I didn't want to do anything that could raise red flags. He never apologized, and never acknowledged what happened.

Yet again, the unfairness of my situation was brought home to me. I'd been attacked by teachers and police officers and now a UNHCR protection officer. To whom was I supposed to go for help? I knew of girls and women who had to offer sex in exchange for a job. My friend Lita told me that her boss fired her because she refused to have sex with him. That meant she couldn't pay her rent. She asked me if I could help her. I was able to send her enough to cover her rent for two months, but when that money was gone, I had no idea where Lita would go next. She had no power.

Because Omar could not pay a dowry, my father tried everything possible to dissuade me from marrying him. He talked about old prejudices, such as Congolese eating rats, and suggested that Omar already had a wife in Congo and would leave me once I married him. Then one of my aunts and her friend Joselyn came to see me. They sat me down and for more than two hours told me that I was bringing shame on my entire family, that as an educated girl I couldn't marry a man who couldn't even afford a dowry, and that was only proving that educating girls is pointless. Joselyn even claimed that Omar had AIDS, something they knew I feared. I didn't believe them. How could they possibly have confidential medical information about Omar? I remembered when I'd told Gramma Kasine that I would choose my husband no matter what. How dare my family interfere? When I was struggling in school, my aunt hadn't cared about me. She didn't even know which school I attended, and yet here she was, telling me to marry someone who would pay my father a large dowry.

Scovia and I devised an escape plan. She came to visit, and when it was time for her to leave, I packed all my essentials in her bag. Off she went. The next day, I told my parents that she'd called to tell me that she was ill and her husband was in Sudan. They permitted me to leave the house to take care of her. When I got to Scovia's, I collected my things and went straight to Omar's. He wasn't home, but because I had keys I could come and go as I wanted. After my first unhappy overnight visit, I had spent the night at his house more than once. I knew some people gossiped that we were having mind-blowing sex, but we had both agreed to wait until we were married. I prepared dinner while I waited for Omar to come home, preparing to surprise him. When he arrived, at first he didn't believe we were starting our life together. He thought I would go home the next day.

We tried to get married right away. We went to the Refugee Welfare Council, the highest governance office in the camp. Overseeing this office was the chairman who provided marriage certificates to refugees. He charged for this privilege and pocketed the money. We paid him with a live chicken. Scovia came with us, all dressed up. Omar and I wore our regular clothes. We didn't have money to spend on wedding clothes, which didn't bother me. I did wish that we had a camera so we could take photos. We didn't tell anybody in my family because we didn't want my father to interfere.

When we arrived at the office we were asked questions about ourselves and our parents. Then we signed the paperwork, and the chairman told us to come back the next day to get the certificate. We knew that couples usually received their certificates the same day and felt that something strange was going on, but we did as we were told. When Omar returned the next day, the chairman refused to issue the certificate on the grounds that Omar didn't have my parents' consent to marry me. Omar just walked out. He didn't even ask for the return of the chicken.

I stayed with Scovia, biding my time, and a few months later, the camp had an election, and that chairman lost his position. The new chairman, Ismail, spoke Kinyabwisha, and we felt he would help us. Omar went to Ismail and explained our situation. Ismail agreed to marry us if we brought two witnesses. So on February 1, 2009, we went to Ismail's office.

This was a more formal ceremony. Ismail had a Bible and wanted us to make vows to each other: for better, for worse; for richer, for poorer; in sickness and in health; to love and cherish til death do us part. When I heard those words, I thought, I'm not going to agree to this!

If he sleeps around with other women and comes home with AIDS, I'm not staying with him! When Ismail told me to repeat after him, I stayed quiet. Everyone stared at me. I said I didn't expect to make these promises. I didn't want to vow that I wouldn't leave when I knew that if Omar were unfaithful to me or abused me, I would walk away. In the end, Ismail didn't insist. Omar said his vows, Ismail showed us where to sign, and we were married. I was twenty-three years old, too old to get married according to my community.

Acceptance by Omar's church was another challenge. Rarely did women in our community keep their religion if they married a man of a different faith. Had I refused to adopt Omar's religion and beliefs, he would not have married me, no matter how much he loved me.

As fervently as I believed in God, I was not particularly enamoured with organized religion. Where I came from, people hated each other for having different religious beliefs or even if they were of the same faith but a different denomination. Even before we married, the people in his church objected to me because of the way I dressed. They preached that we should all love one another and yet rejected me because I worshipped God in a different way. They wanted him to marry a Seventh-day Adventist girl in a big church wedding with a reception. Maybe they would have been more accepting of me if we had married that way, but we couldn't afford the expense.

When the church learned about our marriage, they demoted Omar so he could no longer serve in the church. They didn't recognize us as a married couple because we hadn't married in the church. Since they saw our marriage as illegal, they concluded that we were living in sin, and Omar could no longer sing in the choir, stand on the pulpit, or lead a prayer. It seemed to me that true Christianity meant taking care of one another with sympathy and compassion. How we treat our neighbours reveals our true religion.

Life in the refugee settlement wasn't easy, and people frequently stole from us because they needed to survive, but we were happy. Our house had a grass roof, and eventually we needed to remove the old grass and replace it with new to avoid leaks. We paid roofers to do it for us. They worked all day but didn't finish the job before nightfall. We slept in our bedroom under the night sky, praying that it wouldn't rain and no one would throw rocks over the wall.

Omar was the opposite of a typical African husband. We did almost everything together. He fetched water for us every day, and we did laundry together at the well. People said I must have hypnotized him with my magical powers, and his friends chastised him for helping me in the house. Omar didn't care what they said. We had meaningful, emotional conversations that brought us closer together. We bought birth control pills at the pharmacy in the Bukere Trading Centre. I tried to keep this private. I didn't want people to know that I didn't want to have children yet. Somehow someone found out and assumed this was something I was doing without Omar's knowledge. I continued my temporary job working as a part-time interpreter and earned the equivalent of $37 each month, and Omar earned about $50 a month as a community worker. He'd help the elderly and orphans to access resources and services, such as housing and school supplies. He often visited the orphans at their foster homes. We were poor, but I didn't care. I'd rather have been happy with a poor man than miserable with a rich one. It's like buying shoes. Buy a pair that doesn't fit, and your feet will hurt whenever you wear them. You won't feel like yourself anymore. When you replace them with shoes that are the perfect size for you, everything falls into place. With Omar, I discovered what it meant to feel like a complete human being.

After a few months, I went back home. I wore one of Scovia's nice dresses. I wanted to see how my father would react. Because I had taken some food with me when I left, I also brought provisions. They were excited to see me and the sugar, rice, and soap — all expensive items — I brought to them. But no one really congratulated me, and after a few minutes my father left, gone to drink at the bar as usual. My mother was more excited to see me again, but it wasn't possible for us to have a meaningful conversation because so many neighbours came by to greet me. Mama and I established a practice of meeting at the market and having our heart-to-hearts there.

We were at home playing cards when a friend from school called me. "Congratulations!" he said when I answered the phone.

"For what?"

"The results are out, and you are among the students who passed." Gratitude for the education I'd received enveloped me. I felt vindicated. People in the village had theorized that I'd lied to my parents and been away working in restaurants (the misconception that women who worked in restaurants or hotels were prostitutes was common in my village) when I said I was at school. Now I had excellent results that proved I'd spent years relentlessly studying.

By then, I had given up on the idea of attending university. I knew only one woman would receive a Windle Trust scholarship, and I was sure it would go to Betty. She was brilliant. But when I asked my friend to check the list of results to see how she'd fared, he told me that I had placed far above her. I jumped around the house crying with joy.

A few days later, Atwaine, the Windle Trust representative who had served as my liaison between my schools and the trust, asked me to come to Mbarara as soon as possible. When we met, he handed me an admission letter from Makerere University in Kampala. I was astonished. At the end of my A-levels I'd filled in the required form listing the universities I hoped to attend, but I had not put down Makerere. I wouldn't have dreamed of it. Makerere was an extremely prestigious university. Many presidents had graduated from Makerere; it was comparable to Harvard or Oxford. Atwaine beamed with pride. He had been like a parent to me, always encouraging and supporting me.

When people heard that I'd been accepted to Makerere University, they were awestruck. Omar and I discussed it thoroughly. He didn't want me to miss a long dreamed about opportunity for which I had worked so hard. But he didn't want to quit his job to follow me to Kampala, either. What would he do in the city while I attended my classes? We agreed that I would go and he would stay in the camp.

Scovia warned me about leaving him behind. "When you return, you will be the second wife," she said.

"I don't mind," I said, but of course that wasn't true. As much as I trusted Omar and knew he wasn't like other men, I couldn't help feeling apprehensive about what this change would mean for our relationship. Omar's friends, meanwhile, told him that allowing me to attend university was a terrible mistake. They predicted that I would meet a rich man and leave him. A real woman, they said, would be at home, raising his children.

Omar and I had been married for six months when I left to attend university. We couldn't afford the fare for him to travel to Kampala and help me get settled. Stories I'd heard about violence and crime in Kampala frightened me. The streets were reputedly full of thieves. Fortunately, Stella, my friend from my last school, had also been offered a place at Makerere, so we planned to rent a room together. I also remembered that an acquaintance, Antony, lived in Kampala and arranged for him to meet us at the taxi park. He warned me to be cautious and not give my bag to anyone. I had thirty thousand shillings deep in my bag — all the money I had.

Stella and Antony were waiting for me when my minibus arrived. The three of us took a taxi to a tall building. It looked like houses stacked one on top of the other, and I thought it would tip over and collapse. This was Douglas Villa Hostel, where Antony lived. We climbed the stairs to his room. While Stella and I rested, Antony went to the front desk to see if a room was available for us to rent. No attendants were at the desk, so we went out to eat. While we were eating, Antony received a phone call and had to leave. He gave us the key to his room and told us to make ourselves at home; he'd be back shortly. Stella and I finished our meal and returned to the hostel, but we couldn't find Antony's room. For half an hour we roamed the corridors of the building. All the doors looked the same, and when we finally saw what we thought was the right one and turned the knob, a man coming down the corridor confronted us.

"What are you looking for in my room?" he demanded.

"We're sorry. We're trying to find our room."

He let out a long, loud laugh. "Are you new to Kampala?"

"Yes."

"You have to be careful. Next time, before opening a door, make sure it's your door. Otherwise, someone will beat you, and you won't be able to remember the way to your house."

Then he looked at the number on the key tag and showed us the way. We weren't even on the right floor! When we got to Antony's room we vowed we wouldn't step outside without him again. We never told Antony that we got lost. We didn't want him to laugh at us.

Stella and I slept in Antony's room that night, and the next morning we rented a room in a private hostel for students with two beds for sixty thousand shillings per semester. My scholarship included regular deposits of spending money, but I would not receive the first deposit until classes started. Fortunately, Stella could afford to pay the first month's rent for both of us, and I would pay her back when I received my spending money. Each floor in the hostel had toilet rooms and a communal bathroom with showers. The hostel also offered self-contained rooms with private toilets and bathrooms, but they were more expensive. The shared facilities didn't bother me after what I'd put up with in the village. A shared bathroom in a hostel seemed like a luxury to me. Unlike at high school, where I scooped water from a basin with my hands, this was my first experience standing under a showerhead while water flowed over me.

It took about fifteen minutes to walk from the hostel to the campus, but the hostel provided a shuttle. I had been walking all my life and was quite happy to take the shuttle. I borrowed money from Stella so I could buy a pair of high-heeled shoes. I wanted to look like a city girl.

Purchasing high heels proved an enormous mistake. On the first day of classes, I put on my new shoes and took the shuttle to the university. But when I descended from the shuttle to the sidewalk in my high heels, I slipped and fell. So much for looking like a sophisticated city girl! I took the shoes off and climbed back onto the shuttle in my bare feet so I could go back and change.

Getting used to the way university worked was a challenge. On the second day, I went to the same room where I'd attended lectures the day before, but this time the room was empty. The lecture rooms confused me, and to make matters worse, the scheduled lecture rooms kept changing. I'd turn up where I thought I should be only to learn that the class was now somewhere else. I was enrolled in philosophy before switching to community development to improve my chance of getting work after graduation. Stella was in psychology, so I was on my own. I didn't want to ask anyone for directions because I feared looking stupid.

I spent countless days traipsing around the campus, trying to figure out the right venue for my classes. The university of my dreams was enormous. It was overwhelming. At night, Stella and I would chat about how we'd gotten lost that day. Luckily for me, I met a girl in my hostel who was in my department. I'd missed almost a week's worth of lectures, but she kindly gave me her notes so I could get caught up. She became my guide on campus, and I followed her everywhere.

Students from all over the continent — including Tanzania, Kenya, Rwanda, and Congo — and from different parts of the world came to Kampala to attend Makerere University. The campus teemed with students from diverse backgrounds and ethnicities. They looked like ants in the ant hills near my village. Some, mostly people who worked full-time and were attending evening classes, drove their own cars. Men with cars could date any girl they wanted. Women with cars were deemed so intimidating that nobody would talk to them. I couldn't help admiring the people with cars. I couldn't imagine being able to drive. I remember telling Stella, "One day, you'll drive a car, but that's impossible for me." Driving, to my mind, was for wealthy people. I believed that if my parents were rich, I had a 100 per cent chance of being rich, too, but because they were poor, I would remain poor.

When my sponsor deposited my pocket money into my bank account, I was glad to know that I could pay off what I owed. My bank was on campus. I didn't know how to use the ATM, so I joined the queue for the teller and withdrew five hundred thousand shillings from my account. As I stashed the money in my purse, the woman who was next in line warned me to be very careful with my cash. It seemed suspicious that she was paying such close attention to my transaction, and I pretended not to hear her. When I got outside, I flagged down a motorcycle and asked the driver to take me to Owino, which I'd heard was the cheapest market in Kampala, to buy some things I needed, including a new pair of shoes.

I was heading for a stall that promised shoes at low prices when a woman came up and took my hand. "Hello, sister. Are you looking for shoes?" When I said that I was, she said, "Don't buy them here. This guy's shoes are expensive. I can take you to a place where they sell good shoes at lower prices. I always go there to buy shoes for my girls. Just follow me, sister."

I had met so many generous, helpful women in the past that I thought I could trust a woman old enough to be my mother. I followed her to a large stall. She told me to sit on a bench at the entrance. "This is a wholesale store. No one is permitted to shop here unless they are going to buy in large quantities, but one of my friends works inside." She told me that the store had a machine at the entrance that would scan my bag for money when I walked in and ring a bell if it detected cash. The bell would alert the owner to a customer, and the owner wouldn't permit the sale of a single pair of shoes. She asked me if I had money with me, and I said yes.

"If you put the money in a plastic bag, the machine will not be able to tell that you have money with you. Do you have a plastic bag?" the woman asked me.

"No."

"I can help you with my plastic bag, and you can return it later."

I took the money from my purse and put it in the plastic bag she handed me. I put the plastic bag in my purse and zipped it shut. I knew my purse could get stolen, so I held it close to my body.

"I'll go into the store first," she said. "When I'm done, you can go inside."

As I waited, I wondered why she was so kind to me. I felt lucky to have met her. I would get my new shoes, and then I would repay Stella what I owed her.

I waited almost an hour, but the woman never came back. I started to worry that something had happened to her. I opened my purse to get my phone to see if Stella had sent me any messages, and I received a terrible shock. My purse was full of papers! The money that I remembered putting in the plastic bag had disappeared. In fact, there was no sign of the plastic bag, either.

I jumped up and threw my purse on the ground. A woman asked me what was wrong. "There are papers in my bag, and I don't know how the papers got there."

"Did you talk with anyone here?" she asked. I told her what had just happened, and she said, "Sorry, my sister, but you have met someone who stole your money using magic. It's the new way of stealing in Kampala, and the police have been warning people to be wary of such stealing."

I wanted to scream, but nothing came out. I was terrified that if I touched the papers, they'd turn into something else. I wanted to abandon my bag, but people in the crowd that had gathered around me told me it was okay to carry it. I called Stella. She told me to get a motorcycle back to the hostel and to keep my phone safe. When I arrived, she was waiting outside to pay the fare.

I called Omar. He wished he had thought to warn me that such a thing could happen and told me to be thankful that I had gotten home safely. The next time, he said, I should withdraw my money from the ATM, which was in a closed room where no one could see what I was doing. In Uganda, thieves loiter inside the banks, looking like customers but watching for anyone making a withdrawal from the teller. It is entirely possible the woman behind me who warned me to be careful was working with the woman in the market. How the second woman replaced my money with pieces of paper I will never know. I remember putting the money in the plastic bag and the plastic bag in my purse, but when I opened it later, it was gone.

The next day I called Atwaine. I couldn't bring myself to tell him that someone had robbed me. I didn't want him to call me stupid and blame me for the theft. Instead, I told him that while I was shopping in Owino, a thief grabbed my purse from me and escaped with it. Atwaine was very understanding. He assured me that he would replace the stolen funds. A few days later, I went back to the bank and got the teller to give me a receipt that showed the balance in my account. I let out a sigh of relief. I could repay Stella and cover my expenses. Based on Omar's advice, I wanted to withdraw the money from the ATM, but I still had no idea how one worked. Fortunately, one of Stella's uncles offered to teach us. After he showed me, I vowed I would never withdraw money from a teller again.

After I was robbed, I was afraid to travel, but I wanted to reset my life, so I went to visit Omar. I spent three days with him, and he comforted me. When I returned to university, Stella had thrown away the papers from my bag and reassured me that everything would be okay. I was very rattled, but once I shared my story with my friends and classmates, I learned that many people had similar experiences when they arrived in Kampala. To this day, I am petrified of being in Uganda with cash.

University was very different from high school. I now had access to libraries, computers, and computer lessons, and I was given a student ID card. I struggled for at least four months to navigate the sprawling campus, but I now had true freedom. No one would beat me for not submitting my assignments or arriving late to class. None of my professors sexually harassed me. The community development program ran mostly in the evening because many of the students worked during the day, so most of my classes were at night. I spent my mornings getting groceries and cooking, attended classes from four until eight, and then studied when I got home. It was exhilarating to live independently. But I also felt vulnerable by myself and was most comfortable when Stella was around. As much as I could, I walked with her.

In the two years I was away at university, Omar did not visit me once. Under the influence of his friends, he pressured me to abandon my studies, and he received my refusal with great disappointment and chagrin. The man who was so attracted to my independence and ambition before we got married lamented my independent thinking once we got married. I would not relent in my commitment to my education. I knew it would serve me well if Omar ever tried to divorce me.

FOURTEEN

The Land of Milk and Honey

In the camp, people prayed day and night that they would get the opportunity to go to Canada. Omar went to church every morning to offer this prayer. Sometimes I went with him, and sometimes I stayed home. If God planned for us to emigrate to Canada it would happen, I said. I struggled with the notion of leaving my family, my culture, and my language in search of greener pastures in a country that was totally different from where I'd grown up. I instead focused my prayers on asking for stability and prosperity for Rwanda and Africa at large. We have so much in Africa — fertile soil, minerals, a favourable climate — but because we're divided along manufactured tribal lines we don't have peace. I blamed the incompetent leadership of presidents who were determined to remain in power forever, but Africa's problems aren't only internal. African nations have supposedly gained their independence, but our bonds to the West remain. We are in debt for money we borrowed from Western nations in the 1980s, and multinational corporations profit off our raw resources. It is painful to see developed nations extract gold from the Congo in the midst of a civil war that has dragged on for more than thirty years. Western powers support our corrupt leaders, turning a blind eye to sham elections and courts that do not appear to adhere to any rule of law, so the public purse is emptied and the voters have little power to do anything to change it. Tanzania is one of the few places in Africa with a functioning democracy.

I used to log on to Omar's email account to check his new messages for him because the internet in Kampala was much more reliable and easier to access than in the camp. On one of those days, I found an email from HIAS Kenya. HIAS is the world's oldest refugee agency. It started as the Hebrew Immigrant Aid Society in 1902 and evolved into a huge multicontinent aid and advocacy organization. HIAS Kenya helped refugees all over Africa and it was through them that we had applied to emigrate to Canada. When Omar and I married, we couldn't afford to pay for a physical copy of our marriage certificate, but we had sent an email to HIAS Kenya to let them know we were a married couple. Now HIAS Kenya was asking for a copy of our marriage certificate.

I raced home as quick as I could and broke the news to my husband. He was happy at this sign that our application to emigrate was proceeding, but he was unsure that we'd be able to get a certificate. The next morning, we headed to the chairman's office with money to pay for the certificate and Mutabazi and Scovia as our witnesses. The chairman wanted my parents to come, too, but I knew that my father would refuse to cooperate since Omar hadn't paid him a dowry. I lied and said they lived too far away and we needed the certificate too urgently to wait for them. The chairman demanded more money, of course, which we paid, and he issued our certificate.

From Kampala, I faxed the certificate to HIAS Kenya. Soon after, I received a form to apply for permanent residence in Canada, which I filled out. I was supposed to include the names of all my siblings. This was a challenge: each of my siblings has more than four names, and I had ten siblings plus my parents and Dorosera. I just put down whatever popped into my head.

A week later, I received a phone call. A woman with a calm, reassuring voice confirmed she was speaking to me and identified herself as calling from HIAS Kenya. "I'm going to ask you a few questions. If you don't understand any of them, please tell me to repeat it for you." She sounded like the kindest stranger I had ever spoken to.

A series of questions followed. She asked for my place of birth. I had refugee status in Uganda, but I was a bit concerned that if I explained how I'd spent my childhood shuffling between my family in Rwanda and my family in Uganda, she would question whether I was legitimately a refugee. I was used to meeting people who assumed my family and I were Ugandan because we had Ugandan names and spoke Runyankore. Then she asked about the circumstances that led me to leave Rwanda. This was what I most dreaded to talk about.

"Did you see a person killing another human?"

"No, but I saw many dead people. I lost a bunch of people from my mother's side. It was mostly Hutu extremists and Tutsi rebels who killed them."

I heard mouse clicks and keyboard taps as she typed my answers into her computer. After about ten minutes, the interview was over.

A few weeks later, they called us for medical tests in Kampala, which we passed. I confided to Stella that our plans to relocate to Canada were going well. I said nothing to my parents because I thought they would try to stop me. Mama would fear she might never see me again. And even though I was married, because Omar had not paid a dowry, my parents had the right to stop me. They could say that our marriage was fake, which would make it easy for immigration to disqualify us. That's why the marriage certificate was so important: we'd been told that the immigration authorities in Canada believed we could not get married without our parents' approval and presence.

I attended my classes but found it hard to pay attention to my studies. A new heaven became my focus. A song in Swahili, "Tutaenda Canaan," said "We shall go to Canaan in heaven." I, like most people I knew in the camp who had this dream, believed Canada was Canaan and sang it as "Tutaenda Canada."

About a month after the phone interview, I was in Kyaka visiting Omar when we were called to attend the immigration office in Kampala for orientation. We arrived the next day. Orientation would take two days, and the Canadian government paid for us to stay in a hotel with other participating refugees.

The instructors educated us about life in Canada. They talked about the Canadian seasons. We knew rainy seasons and dry seasons. Trying to imagine spring, summer, fall, and winter was hard. We anticipated that we'd travel in a few months and imagined that it could be as cold as fifteen degrees Celsius when we'd arrive! That number is so laughable now. They said it would feel like a freezer. Having never seen a freezer, that meant nothing to me.

To my shock, I learned that same-sex marriage was legal. Such a thing was unthinkable in Uganda, which as recently as 2023 passed a law criminalizing LGBTQ+ relationships and any efforts to promote them. Even a joke about homosexual relations can result in violence. I had no problem understanding that someone could be attracted to their own sex. People should be able to use their bodies any way they like, and so long as they are grown up and can decide for themselves, it wasn't for me to judge. I was happy to learn that men were not allowed to beat women or children. When I looked around the room at the other attendees, I saw women beaming with smiles. In that moment, I fell in love with Canada.

Omar and I had a neighbour, Mama Rachel, whose husband, Shelton, beat her almost every night. No one dared say anything. Listening to the violence one night, I was tempted to burst through their door, confront Shelton, and stop him from beating her. Omar held me back. "Shelton said if you step in his door to help Mama Rachel, you'll not leave the house with your neck." And so I did nothing. Listening to the instructor at the orientation, I hoped Mama Rachel would get the chance to relocate to a place where domestic abuse was forbidden.

I felt sick before and during the orientation, and I had a sneaking suspicion that I knew why. Omar and I went to a clinic for a pregnancy test. It cost us five thousand shillings. I produced a urine sample and within ten minutes the smiling nurse said, "You are pregnant!" I didn't want to believe him, not because I wouldn't have been happy to have a baby, but we'd been told that Canada wouldn't allow pregnant women to board the plane, as flying is risky to mother and baby. Omar and I went to a different clinic, paid for a second test, and soon a second nurse announced, "You are pregnant!" I was two months along. We prayed and decided not to say anything. We'd already passed the medical tests and now had only to wait for our Canadian visas.

On October 25, 2010, the International Organization for Migration called to tell us that we had received our visas. We would leave for Canada in just a few days. I let my parents know that Omar and I would come to see them that evening. My parents, of course, had already heard rumours in the village that we were planning to emigrate.

This was the first time Omar had visited my family home as my husband. All my siblings were at my parents' house, and they threw a small party for us. I appreciated that they welcomed my husband so warmly.

After we ate, I broke the news that we were leaving for Canada in three days. Mama immediately rushed out of the house, sobbing. She pleaded with me not to go. She reminded me what had happened to my paternal grandmother.

"This is the end! This is the end!" she cried. "I know I will not see you again. I was very proud of you when you graduated from school. Now you are going. You will not know how I shall die, and I thought you would be the one to bury me." Her words pierced my heart, and I became emotional as well.

"Mama, remember my journey through the forest and the refugee camp in Tanzania. If the Lord protected me during those times when I had lost all hope of seeing you, he will protect me now. We will see each other again. I promise to visit you at the end of the year."

"I will be dead before you return, my daughter."

I tried my best to comfort her. Eventually, she accepted that it was time for me to start my own family. When we returned home, I chose some of our belongings to send to my parents, including my school picture album. I wanted her to be able to see my face whenever she wanted. We gave the rest of the things that we wouldn't take with us to our neighbours. We sold our house for the equivalent of around a hundred dollars.

The next morning, we rode to Kampala in a taxi. I felt so sick during the ride that I wanted to throw up. The immigration office had paid for a hotel room for us. I felt the kind of nausea and exhaustion that only pregnant women feel and, having arranged for Stella to come to our hotel to see us, asked her to bring me some soda. I'd developed a craving for Mirinda, I always loved the grape one particularly, and every day Omar had a bottle of it waiting on the table for me.

We went to the International Organization for Migration (IOM) to get our predeparture medications. This was a requirement for emigration to Canada. We didn't ask why; we were too excited and anxious to make sure everything went smoothly. I dreaded this part. In my experience, medicine in Uganda invariably tasted awful, and I always asked if I could get an injection instead of swallowing a pill or a liquid. Now, of course, I also feared that the medication would harm the baby, but I worried that if I told them about my pregnancy, they would revoke my eligibility. Omar went first, and when it was my turn, I told the doctor the truth.

"You're lucky!" he said. "Normally, if you are pregnant, you can't go. But since you got pregnant after your initial medical checkup, you are free to go." To my added relief, I didn't have to take the medication.

When I returned to Omar, my broad smile told Omar that everything was fine. "We are going! We are going!" I said, and he hugged me.

We'd be leaving the following Tuesday on a flight scheduled for eleven o'clock that night. I spent the weekend with Stella, sharing stories and memories. I gave her my bank card so she could access the funds that remained in my account, and also my phone. We'd shared everything together during our days on campus together, and she was always so kind to me. I wished I could fit her in my suitcase.

On Tuesday, we dressed in our new clothes. We wanted to look like Canadians. I wore a red shirt, fitted jeans, and a pair of black, open-toed shoes. I braided my hair with a pencil, and it looked like I had Ghanaian cornrows. Omar wore a black T-shirt, jeans, and Timberland boots. We boarded an IOM minivan filled with refugees from different camps, single people, married couples, and families from Somalia, Congo, and Sudan, all going to Canada. You could see the joy on our faces and smell the newness of our clothes. I noticed that some people had forgotten to remove the price tags! As we rode to the airport, I mentally scanned through the pages of my life, excited about the new page I was beginning.

To our surprise and joy, we found a group of friends waiting for us at the airport. Omar's friend Momembo had taken a motorcycle to bid us farewell. Stella and her brother, Ntaganda, and some other friends from university were also waiting for us. We hugged and cried. I felt like I was leaving another family behind.

We left our friends and assembled at the IOM desk. Each refugee or family was called forward and given a white plastic bag containing their travel documents, including our single journey document and medical records. "This is your life," the IOM worker told us. "If you lose it, you'll be back in Uganda."

Omar and I had a big suitcase that we had bought especially. I didn't understand how we could hand over the suitcase in Uganda and get it back in Toronto. Next we proceeded to the screening area. As soon as my carry-on bag entered the X-ray machine, the operator said, "You are not taking mangoes on your flight."

"But I'll be hungry. Our journey is almost two days. If I don't eat, I'll die. And I'm pregnant!"

"Don't worry," he assured me. "There's food on the plane for you." And he took the mangoes out of my bag and threw them in the garbage. Why would anyone throw away perfectly good mangoes? I wondered.

We sat in the departure area taking turns holding the precious white plastic bag. Finally, we heard our flight was ready to board. I peered through the airport window at an enormous KLM jet. "I think that's the plane," I said to Omar. At home, I had seen planes going through the clouds and often thought that I would like to fly in one, but when I saw the huge plane waiting at the gate I wondered how it could possibly fly without falling to the ground. Everything seemed like a dream to me. I would be only the second person in my family, after my grandmother, to step on a plane.

We boarded the plane and, like people who had just boarded a plane for the first time and had no idea of the protocol, sat down in two seats. Then a young man stopped in the aisle next to me. "This is my seat," he said.

"I was here before you," I replied.

"Please stand up and find your seat."

I refused to move until a flight attendant in a blue uniform came down the aisle, looked at my boarding pass, and showed me the number and letter that told me which row and seat to sit in, and Omar and I moved to our assigned seats. I had to ask for help fastening the seatbelt, which was buckled so tightly over my lower abdomen that I thought the baby would come out. I felt trapped.

I watched the safety demonstration without understanding what the flight attendant was talking about or why we'd need this information. If the plane crashed, I thought, we'd all be dead. What was the point of the oxygen mask? Everyone else seemed calm and comfortable, but I was sweating in fear. The flight attendants in their blue uniforms and beautiful shoes moved efficiently up and down the aisles. Again and again I stood up hoping to see who would be flying the plane.

And then the plane started to move, slowly at first, like a car. I had not expected that. After ten minutes of driving and gaining speed, the plane suddenly pointed upwards, and I felt my insides drop. I closed my eyes tightly.

"Look at the clouds!" Omar exclaimed.

"Don't tell me we're inside the clouds, please!"

"Open your eyes. It's fun! I wish I had a camera to take pictures."

I opened first one eye and then the other. Passengers were walking around. That seemed crazy to me. "Can you walk in the plane when it's in motion?" I asked Omar. "Where are they going?"

"I think they're going to the toilet."

"There's a toilet on the plane?"

"Yes."

I tried to grasp the concept. "Maybe there is a hole that drops poop out, and it flies in the sky," I said. I prayed that I would never need to use the toilet.

When it was time to eat, the flight attendant came to ask for our preferred meal. I asked for ugari, rice, beans, and chicken. When I received my plate, it wasn't what I was expecting.

"I ordered ugari, rice, beans, and chicken," I said. The confused flight attendant asked me to repeat myself. "Ugari, rice, beans, and chicken," I said again.

"We don't have that, ma'am."

I removed the plastic cover from my dish. "It smells good," Omar said. It looked good, too, but without salt, it tasted bland.

I soon realized that I had no choice: I had to go, and the situation was becoming desperate. I removed my shoes so I wouldn't trip and fall on anyone and then moved like a turtle down the aisle.

When I got inside the tiny space, I did not see anything that looked like the pit toilets in Uganda. I saw something that looked like a basin with water in it, which I thought was for washing my face. I needed to pee. Finally, I pulled down my jeans, sat on the basin, and peed. When I was done, I tried to open the door. I pushed, I pulled, I struggled. Nothing worked. I could hear a man outside the door speaking in English, but I was so focused on my futile attempts to get the door opened that I paid no attention to what he was saying. Perhaps God saw fit to intervene on my behalf because at that point the door magically opened. When I stepped out, it seemed like everyone on the plane was looking at me. I think they realized I had never been on a plane before.

The pilot announced that we were about to land in Amsterdam and everyone fastened their seatbelts again. My ears burned painfully as the plane descended. I thought I'd go deaf. A wave of panic swept over me as the landing gear came down. I had no idea what the noise was and thought a piece of the plane had fallen off. Then I felt a jolt and realized we were on the ground. We'd made it! I sighed with relief and whispered a prayer of thanks.

Amsterdam was cold. I had once lived in the forest, but it was never *that* cold. A woman from IOM guided us through the airport to wait for our flight to Toronto.

The trip to Toronto was not as eventful as the first leg of the journey. I wasn't nearly as scared for this second trip. We arrived in Toronto in the evening after twenty-one hours of travelling. At long last, we had reached the land of milk and honey.

I hoped to be able to stay on the plane long enough to see the pilot, but the flight attendants asked us to depart. I was eager to see the Toronto airport. I'd learned in geography that it was one of the best in Canada.

When we reached the walkway, we could choose to use either stairs or an escalator to go up to the next level. I had never had the chance to use an escalator and wanted to try it, but I feared falling. Two women walking with us attempted it. First one fell, and when the other tried to help her to her feet, they both fell. I wanted to laugh, but during our orientation, we were warned that in Canada people might call the police if you laugh at them or make fun of the way they look, so I covered my mouth and my eyes watered. I used the stairs.

The Toronto airport was huge and filled with people. Women with signs that read "Welcome to Canada!" were waiting to greet us. Our luggage arrived late, but that didn't trouble me. I might have asked about it, but I could tell the workers were very busy, and we had our most crucial piece: the white plastic bag. The immigration officers gave us winter jackets and boots, which I've kept to this day.

We were lodged in a beautiful hotel. Our room had a full-length mirror and crisp white sheets on the bed. The water tap in the bathroom had a motion sensor. I tested the shower, and the water flowed like rain. I knew from orientation that blue meant cold water and red meant hot. I tried both. Wonderful!

Our room had a coffee maker and supplies, so I made coffee, thinking it would taste sweet like Ugandan coffee. I was wrong. It had the bitter taste of the medicine I so hated taking in Uganda. I found out later that in North America, pills are coated with sweet stuff to make them easier to swallow. They don't do that in Uganda. I didn't know if Canadians did anything to make their coffee easier to swallow, but I spat mine into the sink. Then I dropped on the bed and slept like a dead person.

The next morning, we took a short flight on a small plane to Moncton, New Brunswick, where a smiling woman with a blue scarf greeted us.

"My name is Irina," she said. "You are Alpha and Omar! Welcome to Moncton!"

She spoke French and English, so Omar conversed with her in French and I spoke English.

Compared to Toronto, the Moncton airport was tiny, but the people were friendlier. Everyone smiled at us. Irina led us out to her car and told us to put on our seatbelts. I hadn't known that seatbelts were necessary in Canada. In Uganda, nobody cared about them.

As we drove into Moncton, I saw dead yellow leaves on the ground, a sign of fall. Every house looked the same to me. Irina parked the car in front of a three-storey building. I was exhausted, so Irina helped Omar carry our bags up to the third floor. She told me that other immigrants occupied floors one and two.

"This is the reception house," Irina explained. "If you want to eat, I can take you somewhere, but we have bread and milk and cookies here that you can eat if you want."

We had three bedrooms, a bathroom, a kitchen, and a sitting room. In the kitchen was a fridge, which amazed me. I had never seen one before. Irina taught us how to use the stove. I was astonished at how easily we could turn it on and off. I remembered the hours I'd spent collecting firewood in the village so we could cook. And the toilet was inside! You could do everything you needed inside your house. It was heaven.

Our unit had its own washing machine and dryer, and Irina offered to help us when we needed to do laundry, since neither one of us had any idea how to operate either machine. I was used to washing clothes by hand for almost ten people. With only dishes to wash and a floor to mop, I knew I'd soon gain weight!

Everything in our unit was brand new. We had three rooms and decided to sleep in a different room each night just because we could. I felt I was living in two worlds. In forty-eight hours, I had gone from a land where people slept on grass to one where I had a soft, comfortable bed. Someone who had had very little food now had food, someone with no roof over their head now had a roof *and* a ceiling, someone with no status now had status. It was an out-of-body experience.

When I woke up after our first night, I felt like I was still in a dream. I wondered if I would wake up in Uganda if I fell back asleep. I felt hope growing perceptibly within me. I felt excitement for the possibilities that were about to unfold.

Irina came the next day to take us shopping for groceries. She told us to choose whatever we needed. It took hours. In the small markets in

Uganda that I was used to, you ask the seller for what you want, and they hand it to you. Walking up and down the aisles of a large grocery store, examining the well-stocked shelves, and choosing what we wanted was a completely new experience. It took a long time for us to examine each item and put it into our cart. We selected meat, mangoes, pawpaw, milk, honey, rice, apples, and butter. As our cart filled, I thought that Canada truly was Canaan, the land of milk and honey. At the cash register, Irina used her bank card to pay for everything. I was confused: I'd thought that everyone in Canada had a card that they presented, but the food itself was free. But nothing was free, not even in Canada.

When Omar and I got home, the first thing we cooked was meat. I was used to eating meat only on Christmas Day. The meat was shared between ten kids plus visitors, so each person received just a piece. Omar enjoyed every bite of that first meal. I was still nauseated from my pregnancy and had lost my appetite. The only food I craved was ugari, but I assumed Irina had no idea what ugari was and didn't ask if I could get some.

Irina brought us a microwave, probably assuming that we knew what it was and how to use it. When she'd left, Omar said, "This is a big radio!" We had no idea how to work it, so we didn't open it. A worker at the reception house had to explain that we could use it to warm food. Irina also helped us to buy a calling card so we could call Stella and my family to share all our exciting news. We drove everywhere. No more trudging for hours every day. I felt blessed, but I was also lonely. I yearned for the community I had left back in Uganda and for my language. Even though the society I grew up in was terrible for women and girls, it was the society I knew, and I missed my culture. In Uganda, I was out every day with my friends. I probably didn't spend more than two hours inside during the day. Now the only person I saw everyday was Omar, and he wasn't interested in going out very often, which made me feel isolated and lonely. I had everything, but I felt like a fish out of water. I became listless from being stuck inside.

We used Google to locate a Seventh-day Adventist church and called it. A volunteer from the church came to pick us up that Saturday. Everyone in the congregation was excited to see us. It was a multicultural church, and the people lifted our spirits. One member, Roger Robichaud, picked us up and took us to church every week, and if he wasn't available, a man named Bob drove us. Other members, like Angela and Ron, helped us make it to appointments and to integrate. They spent a lot of time with us.

We were fortunate to find a church that became our family in Canada at a time when we couldn't help feeling isolated. Our church warmly welcomed everyone regardless of skin colour or social status. They treated us with love. It was so different from Omar's church in Uganda. Every time I asked for help, someone willingly responded. Kerstin, Joan, and Angela tried their best to make us feel at home. Their selfless acts touched me deeply. I knew that God, the only one who sees our hearts, would reward them. Kerstin would drive an hour from where she lived into Moncton to help me. She made me feel truly loved.

We stayed in the reception house for four weeks and then found a two-bedroom apartment nearby. I was able to sign up with a family doctor. I was pleasantly surprised to learn that I could see my doctor or go to the hospital and not have to pay for the treatment I received. I saw the doctor once a month. I was supposed to take a prenatal vitamin each day, but I hated swallowing pills too much. I didn't worry, because every doctor's appointment confirmed that the pregnancy was going well. Each month I received a milk card, so our fridge was always full of milk for the baby growing inside me. A friend brought us a bottle of honey every month. When I spoke to Stella, I could truly tell her that we were living in the land of milk and honey.

I attended a workshop for pregnant women and learned that I should eat animal protein with every meal, and I ate everything listed:

chicken, beef, rice, fish, and beans, and at least one cup of milk a day. Because we were refugees, the federal government paid for our food and our rent.

Our new life wasn't without its challenges. The government required me to take an English proficiency test, which I had no trouble passing. I decided to make an appointment to take the French test, too. I had never spoken, read, or written French in my life, but Omar was fluent in French. I studied a little and thought I was ready. I took the bus to the test centre, waited in a long queue for my turn, received my test paper, and took my seat.

I looked at the test and couldn't even figure out where to write my name. All the letters were strange to me. I stood up and handed in a blank sheet and waited for a bus to take me home. I knew my house number, but between leftover nervousness from the testing experience and my perception that everything outside looked the same — I heard stories from fellow immigrants about how all houses and buildings in Canada looked the same to them — I missed my stop. I sat in my seat as the driver followed his route and people got on and off. For one hour, two hours, three hours I rode the route over and over. I didn't want to reveal my dilemma to the driver. I don't know what he thought. I didn't have a phone, so I couldn't call Omar, but I knew he must have been worried. I realized that if I didn't return home, Omar might call the police to report me missing, so I finally summoned my courage and approached the driver.

"I can't find my apartment," I said.

"Do you know your address?"

"Yes! Number five Anne Street."

"We've passed there many times. I'll tell you the next time we reach there."

When the bus reached my stop, the driver told me. As I stepped onto the sidewalk in front of our apartment building, I could see Omar at the window, watching for me. I entered our apartment laughing hard at myself and told Omar what had happened. He had been worried about me, but when he heard my story, he had a good laugh, too.

"Do you remember the last time I returned home very late at night?" he asked. I nodded. "I lied to you about going to the African store to get some ugari. I lost my way coming home, but I didn't want to share the story with you because I knew you would laugh at me. I got off at the wrong bus stop and entered another building, thinking it was ours! When I realized it wasn't our house, I went back out and told a lady passing by that I was lost. When she asked what my address was, I drew a blank and couldn't recall anything. The lady said she couldn't help me, but she would call the police, and they would help. When the police showed up, I still couldn't produce our home address. I told the policeman that I was barely a month old in Canada and that I lived close to the reception house. Luckily the police officer knew the reception house. I got into his car, and he brought me home. When we got here, I told him that I recognized the building. He volunteered to walk me in, but I begged him not to and told him not to worry. Can you imagine coming home with a policeman?"

I laughed so hard at Omar's story that I rolled on the floor.

"This is why I never wanted to share the story with you in the first place!" he protested. "If you hadn't told me your story of getting lost today, I would never have shared this with you. You'll tell everyone what happened!"

I couldn't help myself. Omar's story was too good not to share, and I come from a culture of storytelling by the fireplace. I used to tell these stories to other newcomers to show them that it is okay to get lost and that, with time, they would get used to their new lives.

FIFTEEN

The Weather Shock

When people talked about snow, I pictured a heap of salt crystals. We'd seen videos of snowfall during our orientation, but it didn't really prepare me. Before winter truly arrived, some people told me that snow was fun. Others warned it was the worst thing we'd ever experience. Prisca, a friend who'd immigrated from Congo, told me, "You will hate this country forever. Even Canadians who were born in this country cry, so you can imagine how tough it will be for an immigrant like you."

Prisca, of course, did not know everything I'd been through in my life. I was confident I could live in any situation; not even the snow could intimidate me!

One morning I woke up and everything outside was white. I called Prisca to confirm that this was snow. If I'd had a camera I would have taken pictures before it melted. "This is nothing," people told me. "Just wait until Christmas!"

Soon Christmas was everywhere: in the stores, on television commercials, and in the streets as people put up Christmas lights and Christmas trees. I loved it. In Uganda, Christmas was the opportunity to eat rice and meat. If you were lucky, you might wear new clothes to church. Our church gave us a frozen turkey, which I put in the freezer. I'd never eaten turkey and had no idea what to do with the big, frozen bird. Growing up, Christmas was my favourite day of the year. But Omar didn't celebrate Christmas, which meant that I couldn't celebrate it, either. I found it hard to think of Christmas as just any other day, and I missed the Christmas celebrations in Uganda. You could have been starving, but at least you would see jubilant people on the street, celebrating and honouring the birth of Jesus, even as war claimed innocent lives in other parts of the continent. Holidays unite people, and we need that.

Waking up to see that just enough snow had fallen to cover the ground was one thing. Actually seeing white flakes pouring thickly from the sky was another. I was home alone, and I didn't realize that this was snow. I thought the world was coming to an end. It looked like the clouds were falling. I actually picked up the phone to call 911 in a panic, but seeing cars driving down the street and people walking stopped me. No one else seemed frightened, so I put the phone down. I waited for Omar to get home. When he came in, he was excited and smiling.

"What are we going to do?" I asked, trying hard to say calm.

"About what?"

"I think the world is ending. Is it still white outside?"

"Do you mean the snow? It's snowing outside. It's all snow."

I felt stupid. Together we watched the snow fall. Now that I understood, I could see how beautiful it was, and I wanted to go out and touch it. Kids were outside making a snowman. Why had people warned me about something so beautiful? But I soon learned snow's downside, and it was enough to make me want to fly back to Uganda. I lost count of how many times I slipped on the snowy, icy ground and fell, and each time I fell, I worried about the baby. I also came down with my first cold. The runny nose and cough lasted for a month.

As winter stretched on, it seemed to me that everyone in Canada spent their days indoors. I'd look out the windows to see if anyone was passing by, but everyone was inside. This was strange to me. I had never stayed inside day after day after day, and I missed being part of a community where people liked to be outside chatting. Some days, the only voice I heard was Omar's.

The cold was so harsh. I often wore my boots and coat inside the apartment. Pregnancy meant I always felt tired. Irina kindly gave us some playing cards, but as one day turned into the next, I longed to go outside and enjoy the fresh air.

Omar was taking an English course. When he got home, we'd play cards for hours. I noticed that on the days Omar won, I slept badly. On the days I beat him, I slept soundly. The truth was, I hated to lose. Sometimes it made me angry. Losing made me feel like I had failed. If my favourite sports team lost a game, I'd fast all day in response. I decided not to pick a side. I had to learn that it's okay to fail sometimes. Setbacks are part of the journey. They help us become better people and prepare us for our next adventure.

Christians believe that another life exists after this one, a blissful life free of sorrows, tears, death, war, and hate. I don't share this particular belief. Friends say that because I don't believe in life after death, I don't believe in God. I do believe in God. But I also have doubts about the Bible, which is God's word. I believe that some of the stories were designed to defend men's injustices to women. So many stories in the Bible favour men over women that I feel like the Bible was created for men. Why kill a woman for committing adultery when nobody touches the man who also sinned? King Solomon is respected by believers, but he had seven hundred wives, and no verse in the Bible condemns his polygamy. Abraham, the father of all believers, slept with Hagar because his wife, Sarah, could not have children. None of this sits well with me. I believe in being the best possible version of myself in this life. When something goes wrong for me, I try to focus on what I can do differently next time.

I had many names in my head for our baby. I favoured Lucky for a boy, and Blessing for a girl. I hoped for a girl because I knew she would help with chores and other things. I knew from experience that a girl could do things for her mother that a boy couldn't; I'd helped my mother to eat and take care of her personal hygiene when she was hospitalized after a miscarriage. I thought of how I'd sing to my child and shower them with love. And when they were older, I'd tell them that if I died and Omar remarried, they should take care of their stepmother to keep her from turning against them.

The doctor sent me to get an ultrasound to make sure the baby was developing properly. I knew the ultrasound could also reveal the child's sex and thought the technician would tell me. But when the scan was over, she just handed me a photo. I saw legs and a head and went home disappointed. Omar came with me to my next doctor's appointment. She told me the ultrasound showed that everything was fine. Then she asked, "Do you think your baby is a boy or a girl?"

"Maybe a boy," Omar said.

"I'm not sure," I said. "But maybe I have a girl."

"You have a boy!" the doctor said.

And even though I had hoped for a girl, I was elated and shed tears of joy. I retained the patriarchal values of my upbringing. A boy meant that Omar wouldn't be tempted to find another woman, one who could bear him a son, and that Omar's family would value me.

Our church had already given us some things for the baby and planned to hold a baby shower once we knew the baby's sex. The term *baby shower* made me think that all the women would come together and shower the baby with water. Someone explained that women would come and give our unborn son gifts. I grew up where women and their babies shared the same cloth and older babies wore their siblings' cast-off clothes. I could not wait for baby shower day.

When I walked into the church that Sunday evening, my heart melted when I saw all the women from different backgrounds who had gathered to show me love and care. They were beautifully dressed, like wedding guests, and had decorated a chair just for me, the guest of honour. Food and drinks covered a table, and on one side of the room was a pile of wrapped gifts. When each gift was handed to me to open, I would read the name of the tag to announce the giver. But I struggled to pronounce the names correctly and finally asked someone to read the tags for me.

We received so much stuff it filled the car, and Omar had to make multiple trips to carry everything up to our apartment. Baby clothes, blankets, a high chair, a bassinet, a stroller, books — we wondered how we were going to use it all. I had promised Omar that we would have four children, but the heap of gifts tempted me to increase the number! Lucky would indeed be an apt name for our son, I thought.

The snow melted, flowers began to bloom, and the grass turned green. It was a surprise to see new leaves sprouting on trees that had looked dead for months. The vitality of plants that returned from the dead reminded me of my life. I had survived the winter and now my life was blooming anew. I was happy. Sometimes, I'd remember the terrible things that had happened to me and blame myself. I'd think, If I hadn't chosen to go to school, the teachers wouldn't have beaten me, and if I'd stayed in Uganda instead of visiting my grandparents in Rwanda, I wouldn't have been caught up in the war. I had to decide to let the past go and forgive myself. Joy filled my heart again. I could see my life as something beautiful, like the petals of the flowers around me.

I started to see the doctor every other week and then every week.

The baby was due at the end of May, but my due date came and went. I was three days overdue, and then four. I was terrified. Finally, in the first week of June, I felt sustained contractions so intense I could not talk or move. I had boasted of my ability to weather any physical pain, but this was beyond my comprehension. We headed to the hospital. I thought they'd admit me for emergency labour, but the nurse said I had zero dilation and wasn't even close. They sent me home.

That night, when the contractions were three minutes apart, we returned to the hospital, and I was admitted. In between contractions, I told Omar that this would be my first and last baby. He could have children with another woman, I said, as long as I didn't have to go through this again.

The nurses suggested an epidural injection to relieve my pain. They explained the side effects and presented me with a paper that said I consented to the procedure, understood the risks, and wouldn't hold the hospital liable if anything went wrong. I could barely read it, but I signed almost immediately. They administered the medication, my pain vanished, and I fell deeply asleep. But it didn't last. The pain woke me up again, and the doctor came in to check the baby's heartbeat. He suggested we consider a caesarean section because the heartbeat was abnormal. Omar didn't want our baby delivered that way. He urged me to be more patient. I was the one in pain. I just wanted the baby out.

Our son was born at around six a.m., a healthy, strong boy. He was so cute and amazing. I placed him on my chest and basked in the excitement of becoming a mother. My joy at seeing him was so overwhelming that I forgot the pains of childbirth. Omar soon joined me, ecstatic to see his son.

We stayed in the hospital for three days while I recovered from my surgery. The nurses changed my bedding, washed me, and took care of our baby at night so I could sleep. When Omar felt exhausted, they'd take over so he could sleep, too. I couldn't help but think of the women in the refugee camp who needed C-sections and died on their way to Fort Portal or the ones who were flogged during labour to get them to push. I could tell that the nurses in the Moncton hospital weren't just caring for me because they were paid. They truly believed in helping and supporting labouring women and new mothers.

They gave us forms to fill out to apply for the baby's birth certificate.

Omar had many names in mind for his son but settled on calling him Isaac. Traditionally, women weren't allowed to name their children, who belonged to the men. I thought that relocating to a new country with a more equitable culture would allow me some say in our son's name, but no.

Many people, mostly from our church, came to visit us in the hospital. Back home, if you visited a nursing mother in hospital, you brought her food and drinks. In Canada, they brought flowers. And in my culture, when the husband came to see his wife after childbirth, he'd bring rice, matooke, and other fruits, and the new mother left the hospital with a new cloth, usually a kitenge. That was how he showed his appreciation to his wife for giving him a new child. Prisca refused to return home after she gave birth until her husband brought her kitenge, necklaces, and expensive dresses!

We returned to an empty home. In Uganda, a new mother returned to a house teeming with in-laws, her mother, and other family members. Ours was quiet. Omar, little Isaac, and I were alone.

I would have loved Mama to be with us. Seeing Isaac would have made her happy. She'd expressed disbelief that I could take care of a baby. Growing up, I was busy with other things and rarely paid attention to infants. Holding them made me nervous; I was scared I'd drop them. Fortunately, I was blessed with a caring husband who had a special place in his heart for babies. Men who catered to babies were rare in my culture, but Omar was one of them. He could hold a baby in his arms all day long.

A woman from Congo named Catherine lived on the second floor of our apartment building. We'd met when I was out on our balcony, speaking Swahili on the phone. She'd arrived in Canada just a week earlier. I'm not fluent in Swahili, and she didn't speak Kinyarwanda or Runyankore. But Omar spoke Swahili and French fluently, so they could communicate. Catherine taught me an easier way of bathing Isaac than I'd learned in the hospital and came to help me almost every day. She also taught me how to cook sombe, a traditional Congolese food. It's made from ground cassava leaves and is supposed to be nutritious for lactating mothers. We got everything we needed from an African store in Moncton, and I cooked one of the best sombe meals ever for Omar. I fell in love with sombe.

Isaac was one of the most precious gifts I'd ever received. He was the reason for my smiles and joy. Every day, I woke up knowing that I had someone who needed my attention and care. I promised I'd raise him differently than I was raised and give him everything I didn't have when I was growing up. I loved every minute of taking care of my son and our home. I sent some pictures of me with Isaac to Mama, and she finally believed that I was in a better place. She also noticed approvingly that I had gained some weight, for us an indication of health and happiness. Omar had a job as a labourer, but when he came home, he devoted himself to Isaac. I looked at my family with pride.

I had a wonderful summer. No one had told me that Canada's summer was hotter than fire, at least where we were living. I was glad to put away my winter coat, boots, thermal underwear, and snow pants in favour of sandals, shorts, and sleeveless shirts. It reminded me of Africa's beautiful tropical weather.

When Omar knew that he would be going to Canada, he learned to drive and earned a Ugandan driver's licence. In Canada, he passed a written test to show that he understood the Canadian rules and was licensed to drive. After eight months of saving, he was able to buy an older, white Ford Escort. Imagining the opportunities that I could access if I could drive, I decided I wanted a car of my own. I did some research and found the driving requirements intimidating. I'd need a valid driver's licence and a steady job before I could get a car loan, although used cars were more affordable. This sounded impossible, but I bought the province's driver's education manual and studied it carefully. Then I booked an appointment for the written test that would grant me a learner's permit. The test consisted of forty multiple-choice questions and a vision test. I knew I'd need to score at least thirty-two out of forty to pass the test.

I took Isaac on the bus to Service New Brunswick, where I learned that I could not sit the test with a baby. I didn't want to reschedule, so when I saw a woman sitting in the lobby, I asked her to watch Isaac while I wrote my test. She looked at me like she couldn't believe a mother would give her baby to a stranger, but she agreed. I sped through the test in fifteen minutes. Isaac and the woman were playing together happily. Sometimes, you need to trust people.

The test was processed while I waited. I scored thirty-nine out of forty and received my learner's licence. I was authorized to drive under the supervision of a fully licensed adult driver during daylight hours. After twelve months, I could book my test to receive my full licence. I could not wait for Omar to return from work so I could share the news with him. While I waited, I rewarded myself with rice and chicken.

I could not afford to pay for lessons from a professional driving school, but I found someone who was willing to teach me how to drive for free as long as I paid for the gas. My instructor came at least once a month. A year later, I booked the road test. I messed up the parallel parking portion and failed the test. I booked another appointment, watched lots of YouTube tutorials on parallel parking, and failed the test again. I booked a third test, and again I could not parallel park correctly. I failed the fourth attempt, too. Every time I did the test, I had to pay for it. This was getting expensive.

On my fifth attempt, my examiner was a young man. "Take a deep breath," he said. "Sometimes, people feel nervous and scared because of the instructions. Just pretend you're driving with your best friend and you're chatting in the car."

Ten minutes into the test, he told me to parallel park while he stood on the sidewalk and watched. Then he got back in the car and told me to drive back to the office. He scribbled on his forms as I drove. As soon as I parked the car, he extended his right hand to me. "Congratulations!" he said.

I got out of the car, knelt on the ground, and thanked God. If I'd failed that day, it would have taken me a long time to save up the money to pay the fee for another test.

Now that I had a licence, I needed a car. I found cleaning jobs online and would clean houses with Isaac strapped to my back. I could make sixty dollars at a single job, and sometimes my clients gave me tips. Then I learned about a program called Younger Mothers in the Workforce that helped young single and married mothers return to work. I applied, qualified, and received an hourly wage for participating. Not long after, I found out that I was pregnant with our second child. I attempted to combine cleaning jobs with the program, but it was too demanding for an expectant mother, let alone one with a baby. In March 2013, we welcomed our son Jojo.

Life was tough after Jojo's birth. I was home alone most of the time with a baby and a little boy. I had plans to return to school, but that seemed impossible with two small children. By that time, we'd been permanent residents for three years and were eligible to apply for citizenship. Isaac and Jojo were automatically citizens because they were born in Canada. The government rejected my first application because my high-school transcript was missing. I got the transcript and applied again successfully. The Canadian Immigration and Citizenship office sent us a book about Canada's history. We needed to study the book to prepare for a written test. I had more energy in the mornings, so I'd read the book before the boys woke up.

We wrote our tests in Fredericton, the capital of New Brunswick. People from different places around the world filled the testing centre. I was writing the test in English while Omar opted for French. I filled in my exam so quickly that I could tell some of the other test takers thought I was handing in a blank sheet. I hated spending excess time in exam rooms and was always among the first to finish and leave.

When Omar finished his test, we sat in the lobby to await our results. I knew I hadn't answered everything correctly but prayed I'd done well enough to pass. I didn't want to have to make another two-hour trip to Fredericton. We both did well: I scored nineteen out of twenty, and Omar had a perfect twenty. I'll admit I felt a little jealous; I'd hoped to outscore him.

Our citizenship ceremony would take place in Fredericton on December 12, 2014. I went to the mall and bought suits for Omar and our boys. I chose for myself a beautiful pair of pants and a long-sleeved shirt. I planned to take a photograph that we could treasure for the rest of our lives. It felt like a rebirth. I learned Canada's national anthem because I'd heard that the judge who presided over the ceremony might randomly pick someone to sing the song.

The ceremony would begin at ten thirty a.m. I fed my sons breakfast but didn't eat anything myself. I wanted to look trim in my new outfit. I styled my hair in long curls and put on my makeup. I dressed the boys in their suits. We all looked dashing. As we drove to Fredericton, all I could think of was shaking the judge's hand and collecting my certificate. I told Omar to drive fast.

"Good Canadians follow the rules," he said. "Do you know you can lose your citizenship if you go past the speed limit? It's better to reach where we're going late than to get a speeding ticket." That made all of us laugh.

We arrived just in time. We queued up to register before entering the room where the ceremony would take place. I'd never seen a judge before. He looked just like anybody else except for his black gown. We all had to stand and swear an oath of allegiance to Queen Elizabeth, to follow Canada's laws, and to fulfill our duties as Canadian citizens. Then we were called up to receive our certificates. Someone in the crowd took pictures of us with Omar's cellphone. It was one of the happiest weekends of my life. As we left the venue, I held my certificate up and read each word on it. It means everything to me. My heart broke for

Prisca. She had come to Canada before me, but because she could not write or speak English or French, she couldn't apply for citizenship. Instead, she will have to renew her permanent residence every five years. She can't get a Canadian passport, and she can't travel back home. I am so grateful for the education that made it possible for me to become a Canadian citizen, but I can't help wondering why, if Canada is truly a multicultural country, the ability to speak English or French is a requirement of citizenship.

I soon enrolled in the criminology program at Eastern College. I was very surprised that Omar did not support this decision. He didn't think it was necessary or desirable for our family for me to pursue an education and then a career; he saw himself as the provider. He was so opposed that he walked out. This caused me a lot of pain. I didn't want to deprive Isaac and Jojo of a safe home with two loving parents. But my ambitions were also important to me. I wanted to dig deep into the motivations behind crimes against humanity and understand how the civil unrest in Rwanda turned into war. I wanted to explore the consequences of political corruption on its direct victims and society in general. I wanted to know why the people who committed these crimes never faced justice. As with university in Uganda, I knew that putting my education first was the right choice, but because of his opposition, Omar and I would be separated on and off for five years.

At Eastern College, I was the only Black woman in my class, and I thought I would place at the bottom of the rankings. I had always used pens, pencils, and paper in school and found it hard to adapt to doing schoolwork on a computer. When I had to present to my classmates, I doubted that anyone could understand my accent. I thought they'd hear me and think I was stupid. My fluency in Runyankore and Kinyarwanda and ability to speak other African languages meant nothing. I'd ask people in school to repeat something they'd said so that I could understand them better, which they often interpreted as an inability to understand English. One classmate never said a word to me until after we had a test in which I scored one hundred. Her attitude toward me changed, and we eventually became friends.

I was determined to graduate from college. If a lack of books, extreme hunger, my father's opposition, and walking for hours in the driving rain didn't stop me from succeeding in school in Uganda, nothing would stop me here. As a married woman and a mother, I couldn't join my classmates for after-school group study sessions. Studying with two small children at home was difficult, but my friend Jacky often babysat for me, which was very helpful. I often got only two hours of sleep.

I loved my program of study. I learned about cognitive therapy, which helped me to discard a lot of my painful past and focus on the present. I suffered from trauma-induced nightmares. I'd try listening to my favourite music as I fell asleep, thinking it would help me dream of singing and dancing, only to wake up screaming about the teachers who'd flogged me in primary school. "If you can't change the past, why do you keep thinking about it?" my cognitive therapy professor asked. "The past is in the past. What happened to you twenty years ago can't be changed." I scribbled these words down and kept them at my bedside to read before I fell asleep and when I woke up, and although I still had nightmares, they were much less frequent.

We had the opportunity to visit New Brunswick's prisons. I met sex offenders, killers, and thieves. One man had killed his wife after discovering that she had cheated on him three times. He was highly educated, and they had two kids, but he was deeply insecure. When he snuck a look at his wife's phone and read a recent text conversation that confirmed her infidelity, he loaded his gun and shot her. He told me she was the woman of his dreams, and he still loved her. "My two kids lost their mother," he said. "Never love someone so much that you think your life is meaningless without them. I wish now that she was with someone else. At least my kids would be with her, and she would take good care of them. I grieve the loss of my wife every day." At the time I spoke to him, I was having difficulty accepting that not all of my friendships would endure. This helped me to see that the end of one relationship created room for another. Applying cognitive therapy in my own life and conquering my fear of losing loved ones were invaluable lessons that have stayed with me.

I ended up winning a class presentation and was one of the top students in the program. The school notice board displayed my picture and name for a week. At the end of August 2015, I graduated with distinction. I was offered a one-month placement to work with homeless people and in correctional centres in Edmonton, Alberta — almost on the other side of Canada! Omar stayed in Moncton. Kerstin, my friend from church, assured me that she would be there whenever I needed her, and she was true to her word. Her friendship to me and her relationship with my children reminded me of the important role of the paternal aunt.

Omar had a sister who lived in Michigan, a fourteen-hour drive from Moncton, and he expressed his wish to live closer to her. I felt that our sons' relationship with their paternal aunt was too important to miss because of a long drive, so in 2016 we decided to move to Kitchener, Ontario. From Kitchener, we could drive to her home in only five hours.

Neither of us had a job when we arrived in Kitchener. We lived off our savings until, a few months later, I got a job with New Directions, a halfway house for people released from prison, and Omar got a job as an Uber driver. After we moved to Ontario, I often yearned to return to New Brunswick because I missed Kerstin so much. But when our third son, Nathan, was born in 2017, Kerstin came and stayed with us for three weeks.

My promise to Mama to return to Uganda was hard to keep. I'd applied for and received my Canadian passport, but with small children, earning my college diploma, and moving from New Brunswick to Ontario, it never seemed like the perfect time to make such a big trip. I missed her terribly, and I worried about her. At the beginning of 2015, I learned that my father had beaten her so badly that she almost died. I sent a lot of money so she could get treatment in Uganda's best hospital. She was in a coma for three days. Once she recovered, I wanted to find a different place for her to live where he wouldn't see her, maybe even in another country, but she declined. She didn't want to leave my siblings. Later that same year, I received a phone call to tell me that my father was seriously ill. Some in the village discouraged the family from taking him to the hospital. Everyone was tired of him and his abusive behaviour. If he died, my mother would live in peace. I could still feel the beatings he'd given me and remembered how he'd made me sleep outside with the wild dogs. My mother lost her beauty because of him; my siblings couldn't go to school. Our lives would have been difficult no matter what, but if we'd had a peaceful home, two or three of us could have received an education. Let him die, I thought.

But when I heard that they were waiting for my father to take his last breath, I hung up and searched for a number for the Nsambya Hospital in Kampala. I told the person who answered that I needed an ambulance to pick up a patient in Kyaka. I said I would pay whatever it cost. They pointed out that sending an ambulance that distance would be very expensive and advised me to hire a car instead. It would be cheaper and faster than waiting five hours for an ambulance to arrive.

My mother arranged for a car, and I paid for it. He was hospitalized for a week. He couldn't talk and needed a feeding tube to eat. I stayed in contact with the doctors, who told me that he wouldn't survive. I urged them to keep trying. He slowly recovered and returned home, although he was paralyzed on one side and had to learn how to sit and walk again.

People told me that I was wasting my money. I dug deep within my heart and knew that it was good to forgive people while they were alive, to help them even if it seemed they didn't deserve it. I didn't like him, I didn't like what he'd done to our family, and I will never have the kind of relationship with him I have with my mother, but he is my father.

SIXTEEN

Heated Water Will Never Forget That It Was Once Cold

In 2018, I received another urgent call from Uganda to tell me that Mama was ill and I should come to see her. Omar didn't think I should go. Neither did his friends in our community, who asked how a woman could leave her kids and go off to enjoy herself. I hadn't seen my mother in seven years and didn't want her to die without seeing me. I told Omar that I hadn't married the whole community and those men needed to mind their own relationships. Nothing he could say would stop me from going.

I began searching for an affordable airline ticket. Someone had told me that tickets can be cheaper in the middle of the night, so I set my alarm for one a.m. every night so I could wake up and check the travel websites. Nathan was only five months old, and I decided that he would come with me. Omar urged me to leave Nathan at home with him. He worried about jealous people in the village doing something to harm him, like poisoning him. I promised I would keep Nathan with me at all times. I would have liked to take Isaac and Jojo to meet their grandmother, but it was March, and they were in school.

I bought my ticket and packed my bags with gifts for my family. I went to Value Village to purchase clothes for my mother. I got secondhand phones for Elijah and my sister Uwimpuhwe. I had a laptop computer for Alan, Scovia's husband. I filled a travel bag with clothes for children. In addition to my three pieces of luggage, I had a stroller and a car seat for Nathan. My friend Joseline arranged for her family to pick me up at Entebbe Airport. I planned to stay for five weeks. I didn't have a visa, but I knew that, as a Canadian citizen, I could get a visa when I landed in Uganda. This was the freedom I wanted: to wake up and say, "I am going to Uganda!"

I asked Omar to call Mama and tell her I was coming. I didn't want my father to know about my visit in advance. He'd tell everyone in the village.

For the week before my departure, I prepared meals for Omar and the boys to eat while I was away. I baked fish, cooked sombe, and made lots of soup and fried beans. I cleaned the house until it shone and did all the laundry. My sons were excited for me, but they didn't quite get it. They asked if I'd come back that evening, and I had to explain that it would take me two days just to fly to Uganda. I promised I would try to talk to them every day that I was away.

When the big day came and Omar was driving me to the airport, I couldn't help wishing that I had our sons with me. Jojo loves animals, and I knew he would enjoy seeing the goats, cows, and chickens in the village. I also knew my mother would be so happy to see them in person, but travelling with young children would both expensive and difficult, and school is important. I told myself that when they were teenagers, I would take them. I wanted them to taste a different way of life, to be in a house with no stove, fridge, or toilet, to see children who lived without toys or computers. I hoped they would see how kids who don't have much in material terms live so they would know that happiness is not about having material wealth.

At the airport, they weighed my bags and told me they were too heavy. I pulled out most of my own clothes for Omar to take home with him. I didn't care that I would have only a few dresses with me; I wanted all my gifts to make the trip.

When I took my seat on the plane, I looked down at Nathan and thought how lucky he was to get to fly when he was only five months old. A flight attendant in a black-skirted suit and red scarf told me that she would give me a bassinet to put Nathan in. What a relief! I'd been wondering how I could hold him for twenty hours and forty minutes.

The first leg of my trip took me to Brussels. As I waited for my connection, I couldn't help thinking about my paternal grandmother. Was she in this airport when her husband forced her to return to Rwanda? The second flight made a stop in Kigali, Rwanda. As soon as I heard the announcement that we'd be landing in Kigali in a few minutes, I started to shake. In my mind, I could hear people screaming and gunshots. I was so terrified that I woke up Nathan. I thought I would have to get off the plane in Kigali, but a woman sitting near me told me that only those passengers travelling to Kigali would get off.

And then we landed at Entebbe, and I felt the familiar breath of home. I loaded a cart with my luggage and headed for immigration. A man came up to me. He warned me that if I had a computer with me, immigration would seize it. But I could pay him, he said, and he would take the bag with the computer for me. I just smiled. I was too smart for him. He started talking in Ruganda to a friend. I told him that I could understand what they were saying, and they disappeared.

I paid fifty dollars and the immigration officer stamped my passport with a three-month visa. Joseline's aunt and uncle and their adult daughter Angella were waiting for me with a sign with my name written on it. They hugged me and welcomed me back to Uganda. As we drove to Kampala, I could not believe I was back in Uganda. But when forty minutes passed without seeing a white person, I knew I was home.

Joseline's relatives had a huge house with two sitting rooms, a big dining area, and a large kitchen. Cooked fish with peanut soup, mashed matooke, potatoes, and pineapples were on the dining table. They prayed before eating, my mouth watering the entire time. I couldn't wait to dig in. They offered me a spoon, thinking that I no longer remembered how to eat with my hands. No way would I eat my favourite food with a spoon. I ate and ate. They had passion fruit juice, my favourite. When my belly was full, I went upstairs to sleep. The next morning, Angella woke me for breakfast. They served akatogo, a traditional breakfast made with beef, ground peanuts, and matooke. Again I ate until I thought I wouldn't be able to get up.

I phoned Omar to tell him that I'd arrived and said hello to my boys. I called Mama and let her know I was in Uganda. She told me that Scovia and Alan were preparing for my arrival. The next morning, Angella took me to the bus station in time to catch the first bus to Kyegegwa. I had missed travelling with so many people the same colour as me. It was a beautiful experience. Some people stared at me curiously. Many people held their children on their laps, but I had put Nathan in his car seat. I overhead some speculating that I was from abroad and couldn't understand their language. But when the bus stopped where people were selling food and drinks and I spoke in Ruganda to ask for a bottle of cold water, they knew that I'd understood everything they'd said about me.

When we arrived, Alan was waiting for me. He came and hugged me. I looked deep into his eyes to confirm that it was really him. When I got off the bus, I put Nathan in his stroller. Alan kept staring at it. He had never seen one before. Then other people came up to look at it, asking me how I got the baby out.

Scovia was waiting for us. I ran and held her tight. Her kids ran to hug me. While I'd been gone, they'd all grown up. They kept saying "Muzungu" to Nathan. He is so light-skinned that even in Canada some people openly speculated that he had a white father. This was yet another reminder of my grandmother's experience in Belgium. Omar sometimes made comments, but I knew he was joking. If he were serious, I'd get a DNA test.

I went to see Elijah, who lived close to Scovia. He wasn't home, but I met his wife and their one-week-old daughter. Elijah's wife didn't know me so my visit didn't excite her very much. I saw that she had blisters on her arm. I asked her what had happened, and she told me that Elijah had burned her with oil. She asked me not to say anything to him or he would kill her. I was devastated. When I went back to Scovia's and asked her about Elijah, she said that everyone knew that he abused his wife, but nobody wanted to tell me. His first wife had left him, she said, because he beat her every day. After I moved to Canada, Elijah would call sometimes and want to talk about what had happened to us during the war, but I always tried to change the subject or end the conversation. He'd been so little when we hid in the swamp and then made the long walk to Uganda. I didn't want to talk about traumas that he couldn't remember, and I didn't want to dwell on the past.

That night, Elijah came to Scovia's house to see me. He was drunk and wanted to know why I hadn't told him I was coming. I told him I wanted to surprise him. He didn't seem happy to see me. He asked if I'd brought him anything. I gave him the phone I'd brought and then told him I was tired and would see him the next day. I'd been looking forward to seeing him again, but all my excitement ebbed away. He frightened me, and it hurt me to hear people tell me that he was just like our father. I wished I knew of a safe place to take his wife and their three children; he also had a son from his first marriage.

The next day, Elijah came to tell me that his wife had cooked a special meal for me. I went to their house and his wife served me rice, mashed matooke, and chicken. I ate little and had even less to say to my brother. It was a relief when Scovia came to tell me that Nathan was crying so I could leave to feed him. Elijah followed me, complaining that I'd left before paying for my food. I used an app on my phone to transfer a hundred dollars to his bank account, but he showed up later that night trying to get more money he said I owed him. He wasn't the person I'd known before. But although people said he was bad, I knew he wasn't. He'd left school at a young age because of our father's abuse and never learned to read or write. I'd been able to pick myself up, but Elijah couldn't do it. He needed help, and nobody helped him. He'd learned to use violence as a way of protecting himself.

Alan, Scovia, and I slept in the same bedroom. They had gotten a brand-new mattress, blanket, and sheets for me. We talked all night. They wanted me to describe how it felt to fly in a plane. They had so many of the same questions I once had.

I was anxious to see my mother. Alan had a friend with a car and arranged for us to rent it the following afternoon, and I called Mama to let her know when she would see me. The next morning I watched Scovia cook porridge on her stove, wondering if I could remember how to cook on a handmade stove. Then Scovia's daughter Jennifer ran in. "Gramma is here!" she exclaimed. In our culture, we call all older women Gramma, so I didn't know who she meant. And then I heard a voice say, "Good morning." I turned, and it was Mama. I couldn't believe my eyes. I ran to embrace her. She was pale and thin. My father was with her, and I hugged him, too. Mama was in tears. "Even if I die at this moment," she said. "I will rest in peace." My tears began to fall.

Mama had come to Scovia's because she couldn't wait. She worried that I'd go back to Canada without seeing her. She also couldn't wait to see Nathan, but he was asleep. "I can't hold my grandson for the first time without giving him something," Mama said, and she went to the shop to get him some baby slippers. As soon as he woke up, I went to get him so he could meet his grandmother for the first time. She immediately told me that he looked like me. No one had ever said that before.

That night, my parents slept at Scovia's house with us. In the morning, I handed out all the gifts I'd brought. Alan had never touched a computer before and didn't know how to turn it on. He was overjoyed and called everyone to come and see it. The kids were very excited about the clothes I'd brought them. Some of them were in torn clothes and had no shoes. I wanted to tell them that I had once been like them. I made a video of them so my boys could see how excited children could be over a dress.

Omar's cousin Peter came to drive me, Nathan, and my parents to my parents' house. My mother was anxious to get back because so many people in the village were waiting to see me, the woman who never gave up. Knowing that I wouldn't be able to get diapers and wipes in the village, I took plenty with me. Scovia worried about thieves who would assume I had a lot of cash with me. On the drive, I learned from Mama that Kasine was doing okay but had lost her eyesight. I'd spoken to her on the phone and she never said a word about her blindness. It saddened me to know that she wouldn't be able to see me or her great-grandson.

People surrounded us as soon as we arrived: family, neighbours, and strangers. Those who spoke a little English talked to me in English, but I replied in Runyankore, which surprised them. They assumed I'd forgotten how to speak my mother tongue. I could hear Kasine calling to me: "Kadur! Kadur!" I went into the house. At least fifteen people filled the room. I started shaking hands with each one in turn, but then I couldn't wait to get to my grandmother. I clutched her hands and looked into her eyes. That she couldn't see me made me sob. But then she gently touched my face. She ran her fingers over the marks on my forehead from the times she'd pressed hot metal on my skin to relieve my headaches. "It's you," she said. I burst into tears, and everyone else started to cry, too. Gramma asked to hold my son, and I put him in her arms.

For dinner, they prepared matooke and eggplant. We all sat in a circle, and I felt reunion, togetherness, and family. That night, I wanted to sleep with my grandmother, but the mattress wasn't big enough for her, me, and Nathan. Gramma said she'd sit up for the whole night and protect me, but I stayed awake with her so we could talk. She thanked God for our reunion. She'd dreamed that she'd die before we were together again. "I can't see your face, but I can still see your young figure," she said.

I asked her if there was anything she hadn't done that she wished she could do before she died. "I did everything I was supposed to do. I am waiting for my time to go. I am not ready, but if my time comes, I will accept the plan of God," she told me. "I never knew that I would see you again. Rurema, the creator, did it. I pray every day. I am closer to God. He knows how long we are going to live. He has all our plans." She advised me to get close to God and ask him all my questions, and she talked about how the world was coming to an end. People didn't care about others, she said, only themselves. But the people she helped as a healer were taking care of her, and strangers sometimes showed up with food. "This is how your deeds will follow you. You will harvest all that you planted before you leave. Love one another. If you fall, pick yourself up; never expect that others will pick you up. They have their own issues. Everyone is struggling with something." I had grown up thinking that my grandmother was the smartest person in the village. She still was.

The next morning, I went to see where she lived. She rented a single small room. She had an old, torn mattress. Looking at her humble surroundings, I told her I would do my best to buy a house for her. Most of the houses in the village were made of mud. Some were thatched with grass. One neighbour's eight children slept on the same mat. I thought with disbelief that I had once lived like this, and even slept outdoors many nights, and now Omar and I had our own bedroom and our children slept in their own beds. The next day, I saw a small brick house with a sitting room and a bedroom that was for sale for the equivalent of fifteen hundred dollars. It had iron sheets for a roof.

I called Omar and explained how much money I needed and why. He did not hesitate. He sent the money the next day. I bought her a new mattress, a new bed, and new kitchen utensils. I bought her rice and meat, her favourite foods. She couldn't see the house, of course, but she touched all the walls and the floor and all the new things I'd bought for her. She saw it all with her heart. She told me she had never felt so loved and that she did not know I loved her so much. She asked if she could dance for me to show her gratitude. The only thing I wanted was to sit with her in the evening and listen to one of the stories she used to tell us at the fireplace, but she no longer remembered them.

One Sunday I went with Mama to church. She wanted everyone at the church to see me. She'd asked them to pray for her that she would see me again and promised that if her prayers were realized, she'd offer God the greatest gift possible.

The church was small, and the walls were made of mud. A choir dressed in white was at the sanctuary. On the left and right of the centre aisle were two rows of chairs. I sat in the back. When worship began, my mother was called to address the congregation. She stood and thanked everyone who prayed with her.

"God has answered my prayers," she said. "If you look at the back, you will see an unfamiliar face. She is my daughter I have been telling you about." Everyone whistled and applauded. My eyes filled with tears as my mother and the choir sang a song to Jesus and Gramma got up and did one of her slow dances of celebration. Mama carried a small handmade basket. She collected money to give to the church for the sake of the Lord. This was how she expressed her gratitude. It was a special day.

I hoped to see Aunt Karuhanga. I had last seen her twenty-two years earlier. Even before I left for Canada, I didn't have extra money to travel to see her, and when she visited my parents, I was away at school. I also didn't like her husband, which discouraged me from going to her house. I missed her soothing lap and wanted to have another conversation with her. Unfortunately, my many attempts to reach her by phone were unsuccessful. Later, I'd learn that her phone had died, and she didn't find out about my visit until after I'd returned to Canada, when she borrowed a neighbour's phone and called my parents. Her heart was in pieces.

Bosco paid us a visit that lasted three days. I was happy to see him, but very little had changed in his life. He was HIV positive and still idle. I told him I would do my best to support him, and I have fulfilled that promise, buying him clothes and paying for his hospital visits.

We were in the garden getting matooke. My mother didn't know that I still remembered how to carry it on my head. I told her that in Canada, we didn't carry anything on our heads; we used our car. When she learned that I knew how to drive, she said, "God is wonderful. I knew your hard work would pay off, but I never thought you would be at a point where you would own a car!"

She shared with me that my father no longer beat her as he had before, but she was still going through the same struggle with him: uncontrollable rage, drinking, and constant demands. He's weakened as he's grown older and no longer fights with my mother or their neighbours with quite the same intensity. He's substituted verbal abuse for physical. I asked about the beating a few years earlier, when my father almost killed her. I knew that women faced enormous pressure to stay in their unhappy marriages. Those who did were heroes; those who didn't were losers.

"What will your husband say about me separating at this age?" she asked. "If anything goes wrong with you, he will tell you, 'You are just like your mother.'" In my culture, if a woman separated from her husband, her daughter was unlikely to get married because people assumed she would follow her mother's example. Before we married, Omar had observed that men married their mothers-in-law: if the mother-in-law was a good woman, her daughter would be good, too.

Mama encouraged me to respect my husband, to which I pointed out that respect is a two-way street. If Omar respected me, I would respect him back. If he treated me as his wife, I would treat him as my husband, but I would never give a second chance to a man who physically abused me. She was astonished when I told her that in Canada it's illegal to have more than one wife. To her, men had the right to marry as many women as they wanted, but she acknowledged that I was lucky.

Everyone said that people who came from abroad didn't stay long in the camp. But the camp had been my home for many years, and the strength, courage, and determination that I possessed came from the hard life I'd lived in the camp. Even so, many times during my visit I called Omar and told him I wanted to come back to Canada early. Seeing that my aunt Janet had become yamfuye a hagaze deeply troubled me. Everywhere I looked, I saw suffering, more than I could bear. I saw people starving. I saw kids who couldn't walk because jiggers, a parasitic insect, were eating them alive. Some had neither parent nor guardian nor anywhere to sleep. These homeless children would show up at my parents' door every morning because they knew I would give them something to eat. Adults would ask me for money, sometimes mothers needing the school fees for their children, but I couldn't help everyone. I bought extra food and shared what I could. UNHCR trucks still brought Congolese refugees to the camp, the same trucks I'd seen in 1995. When would the displacement stop? Omar told me to ignore the pleas for help; Kerstin generously sent me five hundred dollars.

My father was happy to see me at our first reunion, but he returned to his old ways. One day, I came home late, and he yelled at me and began to hit me. That night I slept at the neighbours' house. The next morning I phoned Scovia, who told me to come and stay with her for the rest of my visit. Scovia's home in Bukere was more than an hour away — far enough away from my father. It was hard to tell Mama and Gramma that I couldn't stay for the final week. Mama was broken. She had arranged a special goodbye for me, but I had to go.

My little brother Nani got two boda boda to take me to Scovia's. I rode on one with my belongings, and Godance, who'd come from Isingiro to see me, rode on the other with Nathan strapped on her back. Most of the family gathered to say goodbye. Everyone was angry that my father was driving me away.

I told Mama never to worry about me. She and Gramma prayed, and Gramma hugged me, her blind eyes full of tears. "I think this is the last time you will see me," she said. I held her as tightly as I could. I told her to call me any time, and I would do my best to help her. I promised Mama that I would be back and that on my next visit, I would go directly to see her. I did not say goodbye to my father.

I tried to phone Mama in the last days before my departure, but my father kept answering. Finally, I called the neighbour and asked her to put Mama on the phone. Our farewell had not been what I'd planned. I wanted to take her to the market and get her anything she wanted. When we spoke, I told her that I'd give money to Scovia to take her shopping.

On the day Nathan and I were supposed to leave, we both were sick. I was throwing up, and Nathan had a fever. Scovia tried putting a cold cloth on him, but it didn't help. I was frightened that someone had poisoned us. I kept only the clothes I was wearing and gave everything else to Scovia. It was time to go.

I asked the driver of the taxi to stop at a clinic so I could get some medicine to bring down Nathan's fever, but he refused. He wanted to get to the taxi park to pick up more passengers. When we finally reached Kampala, I left my bags in the taxi and rushed through the rain in search of a clinic. Despite the rain, the streets were jammed with people. Nathan was on my back, sweating, and I carried his diaper bag with my passport and some money in it. My shoes were covered in mud. I asked where the nearest clinic was, and nobody answered me. I shouted that my baby was dying, and nobody cared. Finally a boda boda guy offered to take us. I paid him thirty thousand shillings, and he raced us through the crowds and traffic.

Fortune suddenly smiled on me; the clinic wasn't busy. The doctor took Nathan's temperature: 38.5 degrees Celsius. He gave him liquid medication and told me to wait for an hour. After an hour had passed, the doctor checked Nathan again and told me to bring him back the next day if his condition hadn't changed. I paid him thirty thousand shillings and asked if he had any other medication to prescribe because I had a flight in a few hours.

"Where are you going?" the doctor asked.

"To Canada."

His jaw dropped. Immediately he told me that he had another, more expensive medication that he could give Nathan. I knew he assumed that because I lived in Canada, I was rich. I told him that if Nathan didn't get better, someone on the plane would help me.

I took a boda boda back to the taxi park. I'd given my phone to Godance and was trying to figure out how to get in touch with Scovia, who knew the driver of the taxi that brought me to Kampala, so I could get my bags. When I got to the taxi park, to my surprise I saw the driver waiting for me. As soon as he saw me, he started yelling at me. "What kind of person are you to just leave your stuff without even telling me where you are going?" he demanded.

I got my bags back, but I knew it was getting dangerously close to my flight time. I had Angella's phone number on a piece of paper, and a woman let me use her phone for five thousand shillings so I could make a call. No one answered, but I sent a text explaining that it was me, and Angella called me back right away. She'd already heard from Scovia that Nathan was sick. She told me to stay where I was: she'd try to borrow her parents' car so she could drive me to the airport.

My flight left at 11:25 p.m. Angella learned that her parents were out and wouldn't be back until around nine o'clock. I had no money left.

Angella contacted Omar and asked him to transfer her some funds so she could hire a taxi and come to get me. I told her I'd be standing on the kiosk opposite the Mapera Building.

By this point, I was famished. I hadn't had the chance to eat or drink anything all day. I stood on the kiosk and looked at the swarms of people and wondered how Angella would find me and what would happen if she didn't. I swore I'd never come back to Uganda with a little baby and was glad I hadn't brought Jojo and Isaac.

I waited for Angella for an hour. When I noticed a girl standing nearby who also looked lost, I asked if I could contact Angella through her phone, and she agreed. It turned out that Angella was only a few feet away. She'd been walking around for twenty minutes and just couldn't see me.

When we got in the taxi, we told the driver that we were in a hurry. Angella kept telling him to give her his seat — she could drive faster! I arrived at the airport at eleven, and they told me that I was too late. I explained about Nathan's illness. I begged them to let me on the plane. Finally they relented. I raced with Nathan on my back and made it just minutes before the gate closed.

I settled in my seat and tried to relax, but my mind kept spinning. Between the bumpy roads, the rain, and the stress, I was worn out. I wished for sleep and for treatment for Nathan in Canada. I remembered that I'd once left him with Scovia, and she gave him some fresh milk. I was angry when I found out, but she said she did it with her children all the time and nothing happened to them. She used to call me and tell me that her kids were really sick and she didn't know why! I wondered if maybe unpasteurized milk was the cause of Nathan's illness. I held him all the way to Brussels.

As I flew across the Atlantic to Toronto, every time I looked out the window and saw the ocean, unwelcome memories rose up. I recalled the dead bodies I'd seen when I crossed the river from Rwanda to Tanzania. When will these images go away? I asked myself. Will talking about what happened help? I doubted it. Who would help? Would they understand what I went through? All through that long flight, I thought about the past.

When we landed in Toronto, I was among the first people off the plane. Nathan had made it, and I praised God for bringing us safely home. I wondered what Omar would say. In the airport, I followed the crowd to pick up my luggage. My feet were swollen and numb. Many people stared at me. Some asked if they could take a picture of me with Nathan on my back, tied with a kitenge. A man approached to ask if I was heading to immigration. No, I said. I'm Canadian, and I pulled out my passport just in case he didn't know that someone like me could be Canadian.

Omar was waiting for us in the arrivals area. He hugged me, and I took Nathan off my back and handed him to his father. "What happened?" Omar asked. "He's lost some weight." So I explained about the sickness.

We drove all the way from Toronto to Kitchener in tired silence. I was jetlagged and worried about Nathan, wondering if he had caught a bug or been poisoned and if Canada would have an antidote if that were the case. I had to take my shoes off my swollen feet. When we got home, I could not wait to go to bed. After weeks of sleeping on mats on the floor, my ribs hurt. Omar said the boys would be home from school soon and suggested I take a warm shower, but I couldn't. I just wanted a cup of milk and some sleep.

Nathan's howl tore me from my sleep. I went to him, and I started shaking like a leaf. I called 911 immediately. The operator kept asking me questions. Fire trucks pulled up outside, and two firefighters with an emergency bag rushed into the house. Nathan was panting. They checked his temperature and then put an oxygen mask over his face.

"He has a fever," one of them said. "Undress him. Do you have his health card?"

I rushed into the bedroom and changed my clothes.

"Who is coming with him?" a firefighter asked. Omar clutched Nathan to his chest and carried him outside. Paramedics put him on a gurney. I climbed into the back of the ambulance with him.

When we got to the hospital and I told them we had just come from Uganda, they isolated us immediately. They suspected it might be Ebola. Every time a nurse or doctor entered the room, they were clad in personal protective equipment. I showed a doctor my hugely swollen feet, and he assured me it would go away in a few days. I told him that when I was little, I had walked across three countries on foot. Could this be the reason for my swollen feet?

"Three countries?" he asked. "How is that possible? I think this came from sitting for long hours and the blood not circulating that well."

I witnessed the care the doctors and nurses gave my son and compared it to the clinics and hospitals in Uganda, where everyone had their hand out for money, and my heart broke for those people who had no access to medical care.

After a few days, Nathan was eating well and regaining his strength, and at last we could truly go home and I could see Isaac and Jojo again. My journey to Uganda had been bittersweet, but I had no regrets.

SEVENTEEN
Giving Back

New windows were installed in our apartment in Kitchener, and a woman named Demi came to repaint the trim. I asked her where I could find a dress for Nathan's dedication, a confirmation between the parents and the church to raise the child in a godly way until Nathan was old enough to decide for himself to keep God in his life. Demi suggested I visit the Conestoga Mall in Waterloo. That was the extent of our conversation. The following Sunday, a man we'd never met knocked on our door. He said his name was John and his wife was one of the women painting our windows. He handed us a thick envelope and told us the gift was supposed to be anonymous, but he didn't want to leave it in the mailbox.

We opened the envelope, and inside were new bills: one, two, three, four, five hundred dollars cash! Omar couldn't believe someone we didn't know would give us so much money as a gift.

When Demi came on Monday, I asked her about it. "Since I've been coming to your place, I've been amazed," she said. "I thought that someone with three small boys would have a disorganized house, but you don't. My friend and I smell the food you cook for your family and see how wonderful and caring you are as a mother. When I went home and told my husband about you, it touched his heart, and he wanted to give your family a gift."

It meant everything to me that people saw me as a good mother. I never wanted the trauma of my past to affect the way I mothered my children, and I'd sworn to myself that I would do everything possible to break the cycle of violence. The suffering would end with me, and I'd give my children and the generations that followed them better lives.

Sometimes I asked myself how I'd give the love that I never had. I had lost my childhood; I couldn't really remember ever being a child. At a young age, I'd been taking care of my siblings and helping my mother. I started with reminding myself every day to be kind, to forgive others, and to forgive myself. I'd get up saying prayers of forgiveness. This didn't mean that I'd forget what they had done to me, but I knew that holding onto my anger and resentment was killing me. I spent a lot of time thinking about the members of my scattered, extended family. So many of them struggled with alcohol and domestic violence. Some had diseases that would go untreated. They were sinking, one by one, and I couldn't grab their hands and pull them up. I know so many people who didn't make it through, girls who, unlike me, believed in society's rules and walked in the footsteps of their ancestors.

I called John that evening to thank him. As we talked, I told him a bit about my life, and my story astonished him. I told him that my next Canadian dream was to buy a house, and he offered to introduce me and Omar to someone who might be able to help. He connected me with Jeff Reitzel, an ambassador for Possibilities International, an Ontario-based humanitarian organization that helps people worldwide, including in Ghana in West Africa. When I heard that they also have an orphanage in Accra, I told Jeff about the time I spent in Kagenyi Camp in Tanzania with other Rwandan orphans.

Jeff said Possibility International was planning a ten-day trip to Ghana and proposed sponsoring me to join them so I could visit the orphanage. This was a dream come true. But I was still breastfeeding

Nathan, and after the trip to Uganda the previous year, I didn't want to take him with me. Jeff told me not to worry; I could go next time. I couldn't bear to wait. When I see an opportunity, I need to act. Who knows what tomorrow holds? I told Jeff I would go.

Omar took some convincing. He argued that I couldn't go because Nathan was breastfeeding. I said that I would move him to formula. Then Omar said that he couldn't miss work to stay home and look after the boys. At that time, he was a self-employed Uber driver. I lied and told him that Jeff would make up for whatever income he missed. Finally he agreed. (I'm happy to say that when Omar found out about my fib, he was okay about it.)

Jeff handled the travel arrangements, and I started to wean Nathan. It wasn't easy. Once I sat up all night because he couldn't sleep. He cried for hours. Omar thought I had lost my mind. He didn't know that visiting this orphanage was a dream of mine because I had never shared with him the details of what I experienced as a child in a refugee camp. I'd thought my parents were dead. I knew what it meant to call out for my mother and know that she wouldn't hear me. This was an opportunity for me to give back. I felt it was my calling.

Jeff had many supplies he was taking to the orphanage, and he bought some items and nonperishable foods. Jeff's cousins, Curtis and Matt, picked me up, and we went to get Jeff. We took our first group picture standing in front of Jeff's house before heading to the airport. I could barely contain my excitement. I couldn't wait to see the kids at the orphanage. For me, the trip was about hope: the hope that I could convince them that their future could be brighter, and the hope that I could be a living example that despair is not a life sentence.

When we arrived at the orphanage, I could see that Jeff was like a father to the children, and he had missed them. Babies crawled to him, and the older kids were so excited to see us that I couldn't stop smiling. I hugged them with all my heart. I felt I had much to offer. Remembering those adults who had looked after me, like Buseka, I spoke with the women who cared for the children about their impact on these young lives. Some of them looked at me like I was preaching to them, but I felt strongly that because of my experiences what I had to say was important.

I visited a leprosy community and helped the residents to clean and paint their houses. I felt like I was painting love into their hearts. Many of the women looked like Kasine.

Giving back to people in need was good for my heart, but it wasn't always easy. We went to a school for the deaf, and I had a panic attack. The classroom full of students took me back to my days as a beaten, bullied student in Uganda. I excused myself and went into the bathroom to calm down and the nurse accompanying us gave me some medication. I didn't tell anyone why I was so upset. It was a struggle I felt I needed to work through on my own.

On our way back, the police stopped our vehicle and said they needed to search us for drugs. One of the officers spoke to me, but I didn't understand what he was saying. Our driver explained that I was Canadian, but the officer ordered me out of the van and searched my bag. Another officer asked me if I was married. He wanted to marry me, he said, and asked for my phone number. I didn't want trouble, so I gave him a fake number. The police let us go once Jeff gave them some money. I wondered what might have happened if I'd been travelling alone. I thought of the police in Uganda, and again, the willingness of police to abuse their power disturbed me.

The trip was an enormous success. We brought joy and warmth to children in despair, and I tasted my life's purpose. I understood what I could offer those in need, and I returned to Canada with a new focus. Nothing would stop me.

From a young age, I'd dreamed of being a voice for the voiceless, of standing up for girls and women. When we moved to Kitchener, I began working with homeless people at House of Friendship. My heart broke for them. I know how it feels to have no home, to feel that you don't even want to live anymore because you're so unwanted that you don't feel human. A lot of them talked about what they'd gone through when they were younger. I knew many who died of drug overdoses.

Some people argue that homelessness is a choice. A friend of mine told me that she had been in worse situations than these people. If she could make it, why couldn't they? I responded that trauma affects people in different ways and that people who experience trauma at a young age are more likely to struggle as adults.

In December 2020, I got a job with Women's Crisis Services of Waterloo Region as a residential support worker. I answer crisis calls and help the women who come to the shelter to find legal support, housing, employment, safety plans, custody negotiations, and other legal matters. I wake up each morning knowing that I'm going to touch a woman's life. Some days are very challenging. I was once doing intake with a woman who told me that her husband beat her even when she was pregnant. I couldn't help myself: I stopped what I was doing and sobbed. The image of my mother lying on the floor, everyone thinking she was dead, was so vivid. Then I wiped my eyes and told this woman that she was in the right hands; we would help her start her new journey.

I began at the humblest of starting points, and a war that I still struggle to understand pushed me to the brink of death. I ate rats and squeezed rotten logs to drink the putrid water. I endured enough in brutal, overflowing camps for twelve lifetimes. I sometimes wonder what my life would have been like if I had been born in Canada. I would have had a soft bed, a down-filled pillow, and blankets to keep the chill at bay. I would have turned a dial on my stove instead of hauling armloads of heavy wood so I could cook over a fire. I'd have had fresh, clean water and a porcelain toilet. But then, I wouldn't have become who I am. So sometimes I'm glad I went through that burning fire. I will carry my scars for the rest of my life, but it won't stop me from being who I am. I know why I am here. It's not to fight for material goods that I won't take with me at the end of this life. What matters are my deeds. How many lives did I touch? Did I help someone to see their own life differently? What can I do to make the world better for everyone? Who can I reach? My experiences have created in me a deep empathy for all people who suffer abuse. I draw on what I've seen and felt to teach others how to draw strength from their worst experiences. It seems like the world's leaders are happy to create wars that hurt and displace the most vulnerable people, leading to mass migration and dislocation. We must be kind to each other and give love to those who don't look like us or speak our language. That's the only way for humanity to win.

I believe in both luck and hard work. I was the first person in my family to attend primary school and the only one to attend secondary school and university and to earn a college diploma. I was lucky to receive the sponsorship that funded my education and believe that God meant for me to have it, but I also know that I received that support because I worked so hard.

No one knew that in 1994, Rwanda would be the epicentre of one of the world's worst atrocities. That event forever altered the lives of millions of people. Thirty years later, my parents still live in a refugee camp in Uganda. They can't go back to Rwanda. Tensions remain, and there is still too much pain. More than once as I grew up, I was sure that God had forgotten about me. But when I look at the whole of my roughly thirty-seven years, I know I was wrong. God has a plan for all of us. When the COVID pandemic began its devastating path across the globe in 2019 and forced us to change the way we lived and interacted with one another, I followed health guidelines and trusted in God.

I don't blame anyone for what happened to me or for what will happen. I draw strength from my setbacks, and when I meet someone who underestimates me because of my sex, skin colour, status, and background, I don't let them diminish me. I take responsibility for my actions and the decisions I make. I am not a victim. I am a victor. My childhood was one of few choices. I knew I didn't want to be married, but I also didn't want to stay in my father's house, and so I chose to endure the hardships of getting an education, believing a better path lay ahead. Many times, I could have given up; many times, I almost did. I chose to keep moving forward.

Because I was born to walk.

Epilogue

On February 13, 2021, I received news I'd always dreaded. My grand-mother Kasine had died.

I'd known she was failing. I'd wanted to send her to the hospital, but over the phone she'd told me not to waste my money. "You've been taking care of me," she said, her voice shaky. "There is nothing I've asked for that you didn't give me. I am holding my right breast, the one that breastfed your mama. Even when I go, I will still hold it, and this will protect you for the rest of your lives. Don't be sad, and tell people not to cry if possible. I did what I was supposed to do, and it's my time to go." Then she told me she wanted to take a shower and wash her hair, and she would call me back. She never did.

When I finally connected with my mother, she told me that, after the shower, Gramma had combed her hair and said she wanted to go to bed. When Mama went to check on her, Gramma could neither speak nor move. I began to shiver. "Please let me talk to her," I said.

Mama put the phone on speaker. I shouted at the top of my lungs, but Gramma gave no sign that she could hear my voice. I realized that questions I'd wanted to ask her, things that came up while I was writing this book, about her own father, Mugoyi, would go unanswered. I kept saying, "I love you, Gramma," something I had always felt but never actually said to her. The room seemed to shrink around me.

I called back later. Mama told me that my grandmother was taking her last breaths. When Omar came home and I told him what was happening, he suggested that I go to Uganda. Even if she couldn't see or hear me, I could see her face one last time. Of course it takes a long time to get to Uganda from Canada, and the pandemic added another complication: I'd need a couple of days to get tested for COVID. I didn't know what to do. Early the next morning, I learned that my beloved grandmother had passed away. She told me that she was one hundred years old. I don't think she really was. She didn't look it.

I went to work but asked my manager to find someone to replace me for the rest of the day. I didn't tell people what had happened. I knew they'd express their sympathy, but they wouldn't truly understand the magnitude of the loss I'd suffered. No matter the sincerity of their words, I knew they wouldn't comfort me. I wanted to be alone at home with my grief. I spent hours in bed. I stopped showering and eating. In front of other people, I tried to pretend I was fine, but I was hurt inside.

People came from all over to say goodbye to Gramma. I paid for a big cow for them to cook and eat at her burial.

Kasine, I still see your smiling face every night. When I look at you in photographs, I don't see you as dead. That comforts me. Again and again, I say the words "I love you," and I know that you can hear me. I am the woman I am today because of you and other incredible women, like Veronic, the grandmother I never knew. I know you are holding your breast for me. Rest in peace, Kasine.

ACKNOWLEDGEMENTS

I am incredibly humbled by everyone who reached out to me and helped me to walk through my hardships. You planted love and kindness in me, and I promise never to disappoint you. You are the reason I exist. For those whom I did not mention here or cannot remember, my heart is grateful.

Gramma Veronic, I never met you, but I will step into the footprints you've left. The stories about you at the fireplace touched me deeply. I will love and protect my sons the way you watched over Dorom.

Mama, you sacrificed so much for me, and I will be on your side as long as I am still in this world. Many times I could not understand why you stayed. Now I do.

Karuhanga, my beloved paternal aunt, your tales at the fireplace helped me tell mine today. I want you to know that I have finished the stories you didn't complete.

Bosco, thank you for being a good brother. Who else would have rescued me from Kagenyi Camp if you hadn't?

To my maternal grandparents, Gramma Kasine and Grampa Mugabushaka. Gramma, my goal was to publish this book while you were still alive. I am trying to be strong. You touched countless lives. After you died, I heard from strangers who wanted me to know how much they'd miss your magic hands. Now is your time to rest. Miss you, Gramma.

To the members of the Seventh-day Adventist church in Moncton, many thanks for welcoming Omar and me. I am forever grateful to have met all of you and for your help in celebrating our baby Isaac. You are all in my heart.

Kerstin and Martin Kuhle, you became my parents when I couldn't be with my mother. Whenever I feel confused, you are the ones to whom I turn. God bless you and your family.

Ron and Angela, I appreciate you for helping us to integrate into Canadian society and especially for taking us to the Salvation Army to get clothes that would see us through the frigid winters.

Jo-Anne and Roger Robichaud, I am grateful that you watched over us and that you sacrificed your time to take us to church every Sabbath.

Bob Bannister and Julie, thank you for your time, especially the two-hour drive to the Saint John hospital for Isaac's medical exams.

Sandra Scrubbandrew, Steven, and Mrs. Freiburger, thank you for being so helpful to me and my family. I am grateful to have met you.

John Stix and lovely Demi, you reminded me that love has no limit. Keep spreading your hearts to the world — you will be rewarded for your good deeds.

Jeff Reitzel and family, you have painted love for the orphans at Assurance of Hope. Thank you for sponsoring my trip.

Francis Coral Mellon, thank you for your giving heart. My family is grateful for your endless generosity. My mother is forever grateful for the financial contribution that helped put their lives back together.

Pastor Paul Casey, Jennifer Casey, Roy Jump, and Immaculate: thank you for trusting us and being part of the group of five to sponsor my sister-in-law.

Pastor Greg Wood and Edith, your inspiring words are touching and incredible, and you have guided me into spiritual life. I will cherish that forever.

Berta Langley and Istavan, you are two of the most amazing people I have ever met, and I thank you for providing education to innocent children. God will reward you abundantly.

To my dad and everyone who bullied me: I proved you wrong. You created a strong woman. I feel the scars you etched on my body, but my heart is pure. It took me a long time, but in writing this book, I affirm that I forgive everyone who thought I deserved mistreatment.

Jill Ainsley and Candida Hadley, my amazing editors, thank you for connecting the dots of my life and making this book possible.

Last but not least, my guide, my mentor, my agent, Chris Casuccio, I remember you telling me that my story will touch countless lives and I hope it will. This book would not have been possible without your effort and energy to find the right home for it.

Finally, to the entire team at Goose Lane Editions, thank you for believing in my story and spending sleepless nights so the world would know the girl who was born to walk, not by choice, but because she was born to walk.

Alpha Nkuranga fled her village as an eight-year-old during the Rwandan civil war of 1994 and subsequently lived in refugee camps in Tanzania and Uganda, where she overcame the odds to graduate high school and attend university. She came to Canada as a refugee in 2010 and currently lives in Kitchener, Ontario, where she works for Women's Crisis Services of Waterloo Region. *Born to Walk* is her first book.

Photo: One for the Wall